DECODING STRATEGY

DECODING STRATEGY

PATTERNS AND PREDICTIONS

Second Edition

Patrick A. McNutt

DECODING STRATEGY—PATTERNS AND PREDICTIONS
SECOND EDITION

10 9 8 7 6
SLP
20 19 18

When ordering this title, use **ISBN 978-1-259-07106-5** or
MHID 1-259-07106-5

Printed in Singapore

To all MBA executives across the world who have participated in class and engaged with game theory, sincere thanks and continued success in your chosen careers.

Nothing is worth more than this day.
—**Johann Wolfgang von Goethe**

Contents

List of Figures

List of Tables

Preface

Games are nature's
Most beautiful creation.
—Leonard Cohen

The book represents a concise introduction to management type and signalling within the context of business strategy. Type is presented in Chapter 1; this does not refer to personal characteristics or personality type, but rather to the indicator of the consistency and execution of a business strategy. Management are defined as Baumol type (Chapter 3), where the execution of strategy is observed through price signals. The reference is to the classic Baumol model of sales revenue maximisation, wherein pricing enables management to apply their strategy or to meet their objective of maximising sales revenue. Similarly, we refer to Marris type (Chapter 4) and cost leadership type (Chapter 5), where an understanding of type is intricately linked to an economic model. Marris type signals organic growth and cost leadership type signals five steps, notably productivity and capacity.

In the later chapters, we introduce type from a game theory perspective. In this context, the reaction expected from the competitor is influenced by the consistency of a business strategy during a game and the reputation of management as a player keeping to type. In particular, the critical timeline introduced throughout the book looks at the process of modelling observed behaviour, by locating a pattern in the observed data to discover its underlying implication for competitor reaction. Using the critical timeline (CTL) to capture behaviour affords management an opportunity to predict the long-term strategic intentions of a competitor, thus enabling them to take evasive action to avoid losing the game.

Market-as-a-Game

The book also introduces the language and some of the concepts and elements of non-cooperative game theory applied to business decision making. Such an application is not new, but the approach we adopt is innovative in its attempt to understand as simply as possible — without diluting its rigorous mathematical reasoning — the game dimension that faces management. In any competition between two players, information is key to winning the game. The market in which the players are competing can be described as a game, and the market-as-a-game acts as a conduit for signals that have the potential to precipitate a reaction from a competitor sooner than the latter had intended or planned. That, in a nutshell, is this book's *cri de couer*. If management believe signals to be true, the consequent action can no longer be deemed an independent action or decision; thus, management become players in a game.

The real meaning of strategy (Chapters 6 and 7) is found in that dark area of belief and action, where information and truth are vital to the determination of strategy. Captured by a concept called the Nash equilibrium, management as players soon realise that the best outcome in a competitive game is not defined in terms of better profit margins, higher market shares or increased revenue, but in terms of the best you can do given the reaction of the competitor who reacts first, the near-rival. The discussion in Chapters 8 to 10 describes the game dimension and offers the reader a strategic toolbox to apply in an everyday situation.

The near-rival is introduced to capture the empirical fact that, increasingly, more and more markets are defined as oligopoly, that is, a market structure with five or fewer competing firms. In such a structure, individual management realise that decision making is interdependent and not independent of the structure in which they find themselves. What should management do? The theory of oligopoly proposes that management take cognizance of a mutual interdependence in the market, and act accordingly.

The Game Does Not Stop

The game theoretic prescription for the sequential games in oligopoly is that the game stops at a unique Nash equilibrium. However, in the real world of business, strategic thinking is contaminated by learning and experience and players repeat actions in different products and geographies. There is a conflict in the literature between game theory and intuition (Reny, 1993). The market-as-a-game concept in the book (Chapter 9) accepts that when one game stops, a new game begins. In our example of Sony *vs* Microsoft in Chapter 9, the price game ended and a new game on content then began. In March 2009, Microsoft decreased the price on its Xbox models by 30 to 50 per cent, and Sony reacted in the late summer of 2009 ahead of the Tokyo games tradeshow. In 2013, both players are still observed as repeating their actions and we describe this as learning how to play the market-as-a-game.

The consequences of our decisions at time period t are more likely to accrue in time period t+1, but the time available to make that decision diminishes in time. In other words, the '+1' simply captures the speed at which the reaction occurs so a decision today can lead to a reaction from a competitor in an hour, today, tomorrow or next year. The speed of the reaction is crucial. The competitor most likely to react first and soonest is defined throughout the book as the near-rival. The identification of a near-rival depends on product and geography. Who is the near-rival to Pepsi? One may reply: Coca-Cola. But no, unless one is describing the geography as North America and the product as carbonated soft drinks, more popularly called cola. For example, if the geography is Europe and the product is bottled water, Coca-Cola is unlikely to be Pepsi's near-rival; rather, it could be Nestlé or Group Danone.

An Intuitive Rationality: Price Signalling

Thinking strategically in the manner just described for Pepsi is at the cusp of Framework T/3. The actions and decisions of management are now subject to conflicting motivations and changing belief systems. Within the T/3 framework, rational decision making is more about identification of a near-rival than the maximisation of a selfish motive *per se*.

Management at company A may be rational in thinking strategically at time period t not to reduce the price of A's product by X per cent; hence, no price signals are observed from A by its competitors — if management is of the belief that company B will react first, and will react aggressively with a greater price reduction than X per cent. The objective of Framework T/3 is contained in the hope of understanding business strategy more intuitively. The rationality of the management of company A is intricately linked with its belief about company B, and this is an intuitive rationality that is co-dependent on the three 'T's' embedded in Framework T/3: type, technology and time.

In a game, any player can regain the competitive advantage with the right management and strategy to find a judicious balance between quality, price and consumer expectations. Players are less willing to cut prices than to increase them. Often, they interpret rising material costs as a reason to increase prices; a fall in material costs is less likely to prompt a reduction in prices. The reaction of a competitor is significant — and there is more.

Consumers have a price range. Demand is positive when price is inside the range: too high a price and less is demanded; if it is too low, concerns over quality are raised. For example, a hotel owner may be reluctant to cut room prices even though half of the rooms on the property are vacant, as raising them when demand recovers could drive away repeat customers and bargain hunters.

Paradoxically, consumers who plan a vacation, for example, respect the fixed price signal as a degree of certainty. It allows them to book their preferred trip in advance in the knowledge that prices will not fall further, as a mistake may be costly. It is difficult to know how good a destination is until you have stayed there. A long-haul flight with multiple stopovers is best avoided — at any price. However, a fruit seller at a market stall who did not lower prices when they were too high would have to discard unsold fruit at the end of the trading day.

The arguments presented in the book are part of a search for that right strategy where all commercial intelligence has been gathered and filtered into a critical timeline. Price wars can be avoided by signalling, and a sustainable competitive advantage has much to do with consumer expectations and the quality reach of your product or service. There should be less focus on the product *per se* but more on the process, which includes consumer expectations and the technology embedded in the product. The latter is driven by changes in the supply chain, economic environment and consumer expectations.

For example, mobile phones evolve to become smartphones, smartphones are differentiated by software and tablets are interchangeable with smartphones. The technology is already there; it is the change in the game due to entry of new players, consumer expectations, adjustment in players' belief systems and technology reach that may have triggered off its implementation at a given time period in the market-as-a-game.

It is because of the dynamic interaction between the players and the mutual recognition of their interdependence that management are sequestered as players in the market-as-a-game to gather information from or to anticipate gathering information from the observed behaviour of competitors from time period t to t + 1. Type is a function of the signals that one observes, and the signals provide management with a key insight into the rational behaviour of the competitor (McNutt, 2009). The real meaning of time-varying strategy throughout this book is to be found in the area of belief and action, where an intuitive and rational decision to act (or not) is mistake-proofed.

In the era of social media and big data, there is so much information to be harnessed. We have outsourced our memory to machines such as smartphones, laptops and tablets. We use Internet search engines and social media sites, credit cards and mobile banking. The preferences, likes and clicks of random unknown individuals are now captured by big data algorithms. Patterns can be discovered in the data. Putting this information together into a pattern allows anyone to predict — with a degree of certainty — what you are likely to do next. It is one thing to know that this is happening, and another to use the information judiciously in gaming, conflict, war, gambling and business. Data has taken centre stage in the information age, and we have been *datified* into patterns. Play the game — observe, but do not judge.

Acknowledgements

Qui desidarat pacem, praeparet bellum.
—**Flavius Vegetius Renatu**

This book opens by introducing management type as an example to capture one's experience of signalling in a business context. Type is a function of signals, and the signals represent observational learning about the observed behaviour of competitors. I am grateful to the many people and organisations who have provided support and encouragement during the past number of years. Early variants of some of the ideas and concepts have appeared on my website and as handouts to executive students on MBA programmes at University College Galway and University of Ulster in Ireland, and at Manchester Business School in the United Kingdom. A 2009 publication in the journal *Homo Oeconomicus* describes a typology for an understanding of type and signals. I am grateful to the editorial board for comments.

I would also like to extend my sincere thanks to the cohorts of students — both graduate and undergraduate at University College Galway and University of Ulster, and at present at the Manchester Business School — who have listened, and continue to listen, to my ideas as they are developed in lectures and seminars. In particular, I wish to acknowledge my appreciation of the very helpful comments, suggestions and case histories received from the present cohort of executives who attend my workshops as part of the MBA programme of the Manchester Business School, in particular: Chee Hean, Paul Ballington, Glenn Carney, David Tzu, Giovanni Genna, Say Khoon Lim, Mark Ross, Ann Gill, Amy Chan, Phil Dunglinson, Mohammed Jamoussi, Waseem Haq, Eddy

Wong, Sandra Thompson, Lim Cher Chua, Neeraj Gupta, Mark Teo, Maria Valle, Stephen Muncaster, Cristina Alamo, Fransisca Situmorang, Kwame Asare, Pawel Biarda, Robert Claxton, Elbert Loois, Patrick Lim, Kenneth Lai, Clelia Rossi, Elena Demidenko, Joseph Tay, Dan Saunders, Tammi Buckley Jones, Olubunmi Ogundeji, Byran McLoughlin, Yvan Cebenka, Marie-Aimee Tourres, Giovanni Genna, Dandan Zheng, Robert Vass, Alistair Benson, Paul Ong and Adrian Migacz. To all of you, may I offer my sincere thanks and appreciation for your comments and suggestions for improvement to the case materials.

My thanks are also extended to the many publishers of the books cited in *Decoding Strategy*, for their permission to include their authors' arguments and points of view. In bringing the book to publication, there are a number of people without whose support and assistance the final manuscript would not have been produced. In the construction of some of the diagrams and technical skills that accompany the text, I owe gratitude to Yien Kwok, Phil Boulton and Xavier Duran, as well as to Gerry Long at Standard Printers in Galway for the production of the manuscript. I would also like to thank Joey Tan and the production team at McGraw-Hill Education in Singapore for their assistance at every stage of the manuscript, and particularly for their constant encouragement and support. I would like to offer a special thanks to the many scribes and poets whose words of wisdom open each chapter.

Interesting books on related themes include the classic and original book by Thomas Schelling, *The Strategy of Conflict* (1960). More modern texts include *The Modern Firm: Games, Strategies and Managers* (Roberts, 2004) and *The Art of Strategy* (Nalebuff and Dixit, 2008). For my MBA students, *Managerial Economics and Business Strategy* (Baye, 2008) and *Economics of Strategy* (Besanko, 2013) are recommended. I would recommend these books for a more detailed analysis of the mechanics behind the strategic reasoning in modern game theory.

In the exchange of ideas, I would like to sincerely thank William Baumol, Shanti Chakravarty, Duncan Easterbrook and Manfred Holler for their specific comments on my papers and conference proceedings, and Paul Patton, Paul Taaffe, Xavier Duran, Francis Henderson, Reza Salehnejad, Jorn Rothe, Paresh Pindolia, Allan Søndergaard, Kevin Jagiello, Bob Ryan and Charles Schell for their exchange of ideas along the way. I would like to thank numerous students and MBA executives in class for thoughtful exchanges on how to present the analysis and for the insight shared across the selected case study materials.

In preparing the critical timelines (CTLs) found in the Appendix at the end of the book, I worked closely with many MBA executives taking the module on economics of strategy. I had advised on the construction of their case-specific CTLs and sought their permission to share them.

The Apple-Rim case was constructed by the team comprising Paul Beesley, Gary Critchley, Omolade Oni, Paul Robinson and Andrew Sen. The Geely case was constructed by Jack Cheong, Huanzhou Soh, Sharon Tan, You Song Tien and Yee Farn Yap. The HSBC case was constructed by Dino Padilha, Fabio Feracioli, Flavio Oliveira and Lucio Rodrigues. The Nokia case was constructed by Liu Juanjuan, Yang Xiutao, Li Le, Gong Lijie, Liu Zhiyuan and Chen Yanqiong. The Pepsi case was constructed by Stefano D'Agostino, Iyabo Elefin, Uzoezi Osagie, Danilo Tyra and Mel Courtney. Finally, the Starbucks case was constructed by Chia Leng Leng, Nancy Liang Min, Loh Ken Ping, Judy Ong-Banks, Lew Wai Lan, Wahyu Qurnia and Pisca Rizky.

The cases are a representative sample of the many CTLs that have been (and continue to be) constructed and analysed during the course of the MBA module on the economics of strategy. More details on my Masters class can be found at **www.patrickmcnutt.com**.

Finally, I would like to thank my wife, Maeve Doherty, for her constant support and encouragement during the writing of this book.

DECODING STRATEGY

CHAPTER 1

Strategic Reasoning

*What we call the beginning is often the end
And to make an end is to make a beginning
The end is where we start from.*
—T.S. Eliot

his book is about understanding individual behaviour in the business world. Rational individuals follow a pattern of behaviour. Think about your own daily routine. Patterns of behaviour can be observed through signals — we can choose to either ignore the signals or analyse them. If we choose to analyse them, we should begin by representing the signals in a critical timeline (CTL). In the Appendix to the book, a representative set of CTLs is illustrated. In business, however, CTLs allow firms and their management teams to identify the patterns of rival firms — patterns that would otherwise be invisible to management. The signals also convey meaning about player type, and players in a game tend to believe what is said as long as such belief is consistent with rationality and the incentives in the game.

Take the following example. If you believe it to be true that Leo the Liar will never tell the truth, how do you respond to his helping hand as you cling for your life over the precipice of a cliff? Do you ignore his help? Do you rely instead on the many applications on your smartphone — so tightly grasped in your other hand — by trying to contact your best friend to come and rescue you? In this instance, cooperation arises if you and Leo — as players in a game — can infer from past behaviour that both of you are likely to be trustworthy. Leo may forgo the short-term gain of keeping to type for the long-term benefit of your friendship. He rescues you from the cliff. You, however, will use the experience to determine whether to believe Leo in future.

In business, as in any other game in life, competitors have a type. The objective of a strategist is not only to define rival behaviour, but to redefine competition as a market-as-a-game. Your best friend may have influenced your belief system with *cheap talk* about Leo. However, your friend is not hanging over a cliff waiting to be rescued. Cheap talk about a player's type is non-binding, costless communication from another player. It is you, however, who must decide whether to trust Leo. The optimal choice for you — as for any player in a game — depends on what Leo as a player believes to be your strategy. Decoding strategy is about less than fully rational players signalling to each other in a time continuum. We choose strategies through a trial-and-error learning process in which we gradually discover that some strategies work better than others. How we behave or what we do creates a pattern — a repetitive pattern — that is hardwired to our game DNA.

Behavioural economics is one of the most active and rapidly growing areas of research in game theory. Most non-cooperative game theory has focused on equilibrium in games and explains the equilibrium in terms of the rules of the game, the rationality of players and the likely pay-offs accruing to each player. The assumptions are that individuals are curious by nature — we like to observe people in action — and we not only like to play games, but also to win. How we cooperate — in the face of temptations to cheat — is an important field of psychological and economic research. Economic research focuses on the tit-for-tat theory of cooperation where rational individuals are disposed to cooperate with each other until one person cheats — at which point cooperation is withdrawn. In time, the cheater will learn the error of his ways and become a more cooperative person. While seamless coordination in the game may be the preferred outcome, a strategy of cooperation requires trust and commitment.

Pattern Hunting: Interpolation

The discussion in the book focuses not only on the actions and reactions of competitor firms, but also on the importance of management type, the role of technology in a game and time. Each makes it possible — and less difficult — to identify patterns of behaviour. The objective is to better understand competitor behaviour with a view to predicting competitor reaction. Our approach is based on the premise that individual behaviour follows a line of action and reaction, thus creating an evolving yet predictable pattern resembling a set of footprints in the sand. The footprints can be observed; the often invisible, often ignored pattern embedded in the footprints, however, is the key to successful strategic planning. As patterns become more complex and signals increase, managing them without a framework becomes more difficult — all you get is a random sequence of signals and you do not really feel that you are in control of the pattern until you construct a CTL.

We work on the premise that a company's CTL is its strategy set as a player in a game. By recording the sequence of moves, it provides an insight into the game and what the player is likely to do next. Management are players in a game; they have a *signature type* that competitor firms need to discover in order to predict the next move in a game of action and reaction, much like a game of chess.

A CTL facilitates visual thinking. It constructs patterns that would otherwise be invisible. As strategy continues to change in a game, it becomes imperative for management to identify and interpret the patterns created within the market-as-a-game. The pattern creates order in past signals by filtering out information that is embedded in the signals — 'taking shadows from the reality of things' *à la* Dante. This allows observers of the game to decode the strategy of the players.

The CTL is shaped by the actions and reactions in a game as well as the signals, forming a signalling cycle converging on an equilibrium point. An analysis of the pattern can inform the fact-finder about the details of how strategy is defined. There are three key observations to note, each representing a basic part of the pattern embedded in the CTL, namely, speed of reaction, frequency of reactions and magnitude of signal changes. In addition, thinking strategically requires a degree of lateral thinking. In other words, there is no yesterday, today or tomorrow. Instead, there is a time continuum in which the game is played and the signals observed. Once a firm — through the auspices of its management team — becomes a player in the market-as-a-game, decisions create their own time — called game time — so that clock time no longer guides the actions and reactions of a player.

In *The Black Swan*, Taleb (2007) commented that you can never predict timing and causation, but you can predict effect. Rather than extrapolate into future time, game embedded strategies (GEMs) recast the prediction problem to one of interpolation in the CTL. The signalling cycle follows probability laws, but "the probability itself propagates according to the law of causality" (Cox and Forshaw, 2011, page 44). To use an analogy: If you observe the weather only today, you have no idea what happened yesterday. Without the patterns, actions and reactions as signals are just as they superficially appear to be — a string of moves devoid of any intrinsic information. Strategic lateral thinking holds the key to decoding strategy.

Strategic Lateral Thinking

In the world of business and economics, decisions are made daily. They are reported in the financial press, and commentary on the financial news media channels is instantaneous. Decisions on product launches, the appointment of new chief executive officers (CEOs), price, costs and revenues are reported on a daily basis by the financial media. The reports and the decisions eventually filter down into a company's performance measures. Guidance from the financial experts is defined in terms of market share movements and profitability numbers. Our premise is that as more and more decisions are made in the context of time (t), the time available ($\bar{T}$) for making a decision diminishes:

$$\frac{d\bar{T}}{dt} = -1.$$

Furthermore, more markets are increasingly characterised by smaller numbers of players whose decisions are wholly interdependent and whose observed behaviour is captured in terms of actions that can lead to a reaction. The actions are signals; the signals are analysed not just by the financial media, but also by competitors in the market. The analysis presented in this book, Framework T/3, offers a template to comment on the observed signals. It focuses on type, technology and time as the three pillars of game embedded strategy.

The theme of this book is strategic thinking. The objective is to decode the strategy of a competitor. This is not a book on game theory *per se*, nor is it a book on the microeconomics of firm behaviour; it is a book on strategy that draws upon basic arguments in both game theory and microeconomics, and it distills those arguments into a cohesive setting called Framework T/3. In defining the economics of strategy, the emphasis will be on management type, technology and time — the three supporting pillars of strategic lateral thinking. Increasingly, competitors are in markets where interdependence has become a key parameter in determining market share and profitability. The decline in the market share of Intel is mirrored by a corresponding increase in the market share of Advanced Micro Devices, Inc (AMD), a condition known as the zero-sum constraint. It becomes a binding constraint when the market share performance of a company reaches an upper bound imposed by the interdependent rivalry with a competitor.

A key feature of a market is that it involves both anonymous and known competitors, opponents with future interaction. Strategy now depends upon the game and the context in which the game is played. The context refers to management and the preferences that guide their behaviour. The behaviour that is observed depends on management type, which is signalled by various real-life situations in the market. For example, if player A reduces prices and player B follows by matching the price reduction, player B could be described as a follower type. Player A, who initiated the price reduction, may have done so to increase revenues in a certain product range. If so, player A could be described as a Baumol type. Why is type important?

In the example of Intel and AMD, the market can be described by two competing firms. It is relatively easy for a fact finder to infer from relative movements in market share. More significantly, both Intel and AMD management are aware of their companies' interdependence. However, in markets with more than two competing firms, it is more difficult to isolate the upper bound on market share. The additional competition — coupled with new technology and rapid innovation — converts the market into an n-player game with entropy. Taking decisions without any information on player type yields a positive payoff to opponents. When one player lags behind technology and the sum of competitors change due to the exit and entry of players, a mismatch occurs between market share movements and the execution of strategy. The game may have been that of Intel *versus* AMD in time period t; the sum of competitors in t + 1 now includes ARM, Qualcomm, AMD, Nvidia and Huawei. The game has changed. In expanding markets such as mobile telephony or Internet search engines, management will experience an upper bound at a point in time. When it translates into underperformance in key financial indicators, it may be too late for management to identify the near-rival.

Observed Learning

Management decisions are influenced by a range of factors — some internal, some external. Principally, management's decision making can be located within the economics of competitor reaction in a 'what if' scenario: What if Dell enters the smartphone market? What if Starbucks emerges as a competitor to Nestlé in the off-site, instant packaged coffee market? What if Apple becomes a telecommunications company? What if a firm reduces price because a competitor firm has done so?

Strategists can look for patterns in the observed signals in order to isolate a strategy set from an evolving string of actions and reactions. Management type provides a key insight into a company's vision, and an analysis of type should be a key component in the strategist's toolbox. The learning of type from signals — referred to as **observed learning** — plays an integral part in decoding strategy. We are not referring to personality traits *per se*; whether a senior executive is aggressive with subordinates or a new recruit is docile with senior management can have a bearing on how a company performs. However, throughout the book, type refers to observed behavioural characteristics in 'the situation' of a game of action and reaction. In the psychology literature, the historic debate on 'person-situation' argues that situational factors predict the behaviour of people much better than personality traits (Mischel, 1968). In a price war, for example, how any one player is likely to react will depend on his player type observed in a game.

The market-as-a-game is analogous to a situation; the game is composed of rational actors — the firms — who are uncertain about each other's behaviour. To optimise his own actions, each player must attempt to predict the actions of other players in the market-as-a-game. The system evolves in a complicated way: When player A forecasts the market strategy of player B, it must also forecast the latter's predictions of others' forecasts including player A, and so on. Market uncertainty exists as players do not know whether potential rivals will enter the game or how they will react on entry. Since game embedded strategy introduces a theory of learning into market equilibrium, asking and challenging why and when equilibrium arises, how we behave as individuals, what we do and how we act in a situation are all hardwired into our game DNA. When a company or individual becomes a player in a game, the game dynamic envelopes their behaviour and *homo sapiens* evolves into *homo ludens*. Hofstadter (2007) best captures a player in game mode as follows: You make decisions, take actions, receive feedback, incorporate it into your 'self', then the updated 'you' make more decisions and so forth, continuously, in a strange loop.

The Game

Zero-sum represents the simplest game, with a long history in game theory. In the classic two-player zero-sum game, one player wins by matching the other's action and the other wins by mismatching. Under these circumstances, we define management as players in a game where the marginal value of their action is proportionate to the reaction of a competitor. This is the Edgeworth constraint, which was introduced more than 100 years ago by Francis Edgeworth (1881) as the concept of complementarity. For example, the demand for cars increases the demand for petrol; if Pfizer spends $10 million on research and development (R&D), competitors will do likewise and spend at least $10 million. Complementarities have an important connection with strategic situations (Vives, 2005). In Framework T/3, the issue facing management is whether to follow a rival action. Zero-sum games allow us to model business strategy in an easily understood manner. However, they have been criticised as being not very helpful as a guide for prediction or decision making, partly because "equilibrium depends on strategic thinking and not learning" (Crawford and Iriberi, 2007, page 1731).

In Framework T/3, observed learning is important in the sense that management observe actions as signals. However, rather than update any prior beliefs about the actions, management engage in a 'I think, you think, I think' loop of reasoning. In Table 1.1, player D observes player A's loss in market share. Player D should also think strategically to avoid a loss of 10.

Zero-sum games facilitate an understanding of how players react to the zero-sum constraint. A fact finder observes that player B's market share increases because the market share of player A is falling. Unless player B has the capacity (Chapter 5) to match the increased

Table 1.1
Entropy and Zero-sum

	Player A	Player B	Player C	Player D
n = 4	40	30	20	10
Zero-sum	30	40	20	10
Entropy	30	35	25	10
n = 3	40	35	25	—

demand over time, the market share gain will be elusive. However, if player B increases market share through its low pricing and player A follows, both players enter into a sequence of price matching that could lead to a zero-price equilibrium: player B takes more market share from player A, the latter exits or acquires player D.

The strategic interaction of prices relegates the importance of independent pricing. Player A follows player B, the latter follows player A. Hence, the players are faced with the paradox of tumbling price. The strategic interaction on market shares creates entropy in a game. Apple's iPhone has increased the market for mobile phones, and within that market there is a redistribution of market shares as a direct consequence of Apple's entry.

Management realise that competitors sometimes do things — reduce price or take costs out of production — that cannot be easily modelled. In Framework T/3, management type is based on a range of variables that can be observed and computed by management, allowing them an opportunity to better understand rival management behaviour. However, in the game theory literature, "differences of opinion arise in assessing the importance of preferences in explaining economic behaviour" (Samuelson, 2005, page 495). Thus, the proposed framework will draw upon the management models, the traditional Baumol model, the Marris model and a cost leadership (CL) model. Later chapters will focus on a classification of types that can be drawn from non-cooperative game theory. Although specific economic characteristics will be identified — Baumol on price, Marris on dividends and CL on costs or leader-follower in game theory — our overall objective is to present a management framework in which management signal their type to the market.

The impact of both type and signalling on business strategy is the genesis of Framework T/3. Signals do convey information about type. A signal is the first derivative of type with respect to time. It allows the observer of the signal to form a judgement on whether the information conveyed is true or false:

$$\text{Type} = f.(\text{Signals})$$

For example, if Baumol Inc conveys a signal in time period t and it is observed at t by Rival Inc, the latter can believe with certainty that Baumol Inc is of Baumol type and will be observed as reducing price to maximise revenue in time period t. Rival Inc can trust Baumol Inc; in this particular instance, trust becomes an assessment tool in Framework T/3. If they are competing for market share, they are in the market-as-a-game and both are players in the game.

Arguably, type can be portrayed by a signal. However, not every signal observed portrays the truth about type. Baumol Inc can simultaneously signal a type and keep a secret (McNutt, 2009). Rival Inc, a trusted competitor, will be in a preferred position if it can read the signals from Baumol Inc and detect that secret. It is in reading signals that an understanding of management type is crucial. Type as a value badge can, therefore, be described as a function of signals. If there is a correlation between type and signal, the game is one of observational learning; if not, it is a game of cheap talk (refer to the earlier example of Leo the Liar in the chapter).

Strategy

Management behave strategically when they understand that every decision is followed by an action that is observed by market participants. This gives us the strategy (S) equation

$$S = PE + NP$$

It is a combination of minimising the Penrose effect (PE; see Chapter 2) and ensuring that one has a response to any reactions to one's initial decision in a game. The latter is known as the Nash premise (NP). Understanding strategy is at the cusp of business acumen, and Framework T/3 explores the possibility that there are three supporting elements in a company's strategy set. A strategy set is a string of moves. Collectively, the three supporting elements define the strategy set, enabling a company to sustain or obtain a strategic advantage in the market. A company's ability or capability to obtain such an advantage depends on its status as a player in the market-as-a-game.

Management are in a game when they abandon independent action, thus realising that interdependence exists in the market that directly affects performance — not just profitability, but also its strategic advantage and conversion into a competitive advantage. The conversion requires knowledge of rivals and an ability to identify the nearest rival, as well as knowledge of the market in which the game is played. Management teams have many tools of analysis at their disposal. The new tools on display in this book focus on observed learning in a market where individual action has to do with the probability of a likely reaction from a competitor. Framing the action — to change price, launch a new product or invest in more R&D — is co-dependent on reading the signals from competitors in the market, observing their behaviour and observing, identifying and finding patterns in the observed data. The initial point of analysis is to ascribe a CTL to the market by converting the observed actions and reactions into a metric.

When Apple Inc launched its iPhone in early 2007, did it do so in the belief that there was a gPhone about to be launched in the market? Our conceptual analysis of **type** is reminiscent of the managerial models with an emphasis on management discretion in a company. The launch of any new product is a company secret. The exact timing is the prerogative of the CEO. The degree of discretion, however, will be influenced by signals in the market-as-a-game, underpinned by reference to the capacity constraints inherent in the production **technology** of the company. Time is introduced by the very nature of the game: in a sequential game, each player has the **time** to observe the actions and reactions (the moves) of the opponent.

Collectively, type, technology and time represent Framework T/3. If the iPhone was launched at time period t because of signals about a gPhone, the Apple Inc strategy can best be understood within Framework T/3. Likewise, in August 2009, Nokia signalled the pre-Christmas launch of a new laptop — the Booklet 3G with both 3G and Wi-Fi capabilities — and, in 2009, Dell Inc signalled its entry into the smartphone market. Ironically, in the early 1990s there was speculation about a possible link between Dell Inc and Nokia in exploiting the complementarities in an evolving personal computer market. Strategy is about understanding the process of filtering the signals in the market. It has as much to do with avoiding a loss in market share as it has to do with gaining market share, and playing to avoid losing rather than to win.

Traditional economic models, known as neoclassical profit maximisation models, are based on perfect knowledge and rational logic aimed at maximising profit. The firm is defined as a single entity with no separation of ownership and control that seeks to maximise profit subject to resource and market constraints. While this has the advantage of being easy to model, it is relatively more difficult to model the importance of the decision-making process in the firm and how it affects the outcome of any decision. Conversely, the early behavioural theories of both March and Simon (1958) and Cyert and March (1963) took into account that management — like any other human activity — is subject to the irrational and is less focused on a single goal. The decision-making process allows multiple decision makers in a firm to reach a satisfactory level of attainment of their individual goals and involves a trade-off between each management group in their individual ambitions.

March and Simon (1958) introduced the notion of 'satisficing', a dilution of the absolute goal of maximising attainment given the limitation of knowledge and degree of uncertainty that prevail on any given decision. They argued that "people possess limited cognitive ability and so can only exercise 'bounded rationality' when making decisions in complex, uncertain situations". This level of satisfaction is not fixed, but varies depending on experience and perception of risk and uncertainty. Satisficing was developed further by Cyert and March (1963), who emphasised the "alternative decision logic — the logic of appropriateness, obligation, duty and rules". Thus, in most organisations, a set of standing instructions tends to dominate in most managerial decisions "rather than anticipatory, consequential choice".

Determining where the final decision rests is harder to model, as this varies from one organisation to another depending on how responsive the firms are in adjusting to their collective experience in the market-as-a-game. The outcome will also be influenced by the prevailing conditions surrounding decision making: Is it collective or individual, a sequence of choices or stand-alone, a single criterion or a collection of less-defined criteria? How much is the inherent willingness within the management structure to obey the rules? By obeying the rules, management keep to type.

Conversely, it may be argued that this adversarial approach to decision making can promote the dysfunctional creativity that Mary Follett (1924) espoused in *Creative Experience*. Decisions that have been reached through this process of collective bargaining may be seen as having a greater chance of optimising the firm's resources and, there-fore, its profitability. However, these multiple factors could also act as a constraint in achieving profit maximisation. Harvey Leibenstein (1976), in *Beyond Economic Man*, had argued that X-factors could also dictate the behaviour and efficiency of the company. Depending on the firm's history of management initiatives, this X-inefficiency can affect the firm's productivity, profitability and size.

What Is Type?

Against this background, Framework T/3 focuses on management as individuals; management can be assessed or ranked according to personality and style, attributes that are personal, subjective and easily observed but difficult to determine. Management do have a unique idiosyncratic style of leadership. However, there is a further intrinsic economic characteristic that is more meaningful as an innate deter-minant of a company's performance — what we call 'type'. Type is a behavioural characteristic, often overt and occasionally covert — an innate characteristic that is a barometer of the likely future behaviour of competitors in the delivery and execution of their strategies.

It is one thing to believe or think about how another individual is more likely to behave. In the absence of any signals, chat or communication, one has to rely on one's belief system. Alternatively, management can observe behaviour as signals of likely action and identify patterns in the signals, as illustrated in Chapter 2.

For example, the Baumol hypothesis is about sales revenue maximisation. One way to achieve this is to focus on price. Under normal circumstances, when price falls, consumers buy more on average and sales revenue should increase. Management can signal a Baumol type by focusing on price or market share. Since revenue maximisation can be achieved using price, it is imperative for management to understand that price not only serves to maximise total revenue, but also acts as a signal to rival competitors. Organic growth, as opposed to growth by acquisition, is a key feature of the Marris model with its emphasis on using capital for R&D expenditure in a trade-off for less dividends today in return for more dividends tomorrow. Management can signal a Marris type by focusing on organic growth through increased capital and R&D expenditure.

Later, we explore types that are located in non-cooperative game theory. For example, there is a type called 'price follower', where the management of company A is observed as reducing price in reaction to company B's price movement. What, if anything, can the management of company B infer from the behaviour of company A? What can they glean from additional information on type? If company A's type is signalled as a price follower — and if that type has particular attributes — what guarantees do company B's management have that the management of company A will subscribe to them at a given point in time? In particular, would they necessarily follow company B's price lead in a game?

In the market-as-a-game, management wait and observe what happens. Because the future is uncertain, the probability that reaction from rivals will follow a certain company's action will be very high in some markets, notably in the oligopoly market where interdependence is the norm. Thus, the value of waiting increases. Management that would have hithertofore acted unilaterally on a product launch (Marris type) or price change (Baumol type) may reconsider their plans. In the interim, rivals observe each other in a wait-and-see scenario. Why is the future uncertain? There are many reasons advanced in the management literature; here, we focus specifically on three — type, technology and time, or Framework T/3.

Trade-offs

In order to understand types of management, we need to understand trade-offs. An indifference relationship considers the trade-off between two variables, X and Y. Management type can be linked to a financial variable — profits, costs, value or sales revenue. For example, a Baumol type of management focuses on revenue and sales maximisation, a Marris type on organic growth through product diversification and a price follower on competitive price movements. Therefore, one key determinant in understanding management type is the ability to unravel the trade-off implicit in the management's decision making. In other words, we need to identify a third variable, Z, about which variables X and Y are indifferent because Z remains constant over the decision-making horizon at t but increases at $t+1$.

The family of management models — including Baumol and the early models of Williamson and Marris — share two key attributes that park their application beyond the traditional microeconomic theory of the firm. First, management are not so preoccupied with profit maximisation which is the norm in the neoclassical models of the firm. There are other variables that attract the interest of management — maximising revenue, maximising growth of the company, avoiding price wars or maximising personal utility or satisfaction. It is the latter that gives rise to a second distinguishing characteristic of the management models — the application of indifference curve analysis to management behaviour.

Indifference Analysis

In the neoclassical paradigm, indifference analysis is used to understand the behaviour of consumers: they are said to be indifferent between two baskets of fruit if their utility — the Z or third variable — does not change when choosing one basket over another. Whether consumers have five apples and three oranges or three apples and five oranges, their utility does not change. Thus, they are declared indifferent between the two baskets of fruit. An indifference relationship can be ascribed to their choice. However, we are presented with a unique application when we ascribe an indifference analysis to the behaviour of management.

We need to identify two variables which management could be indifferent to, such as profits and market share or profits and annualised sales revenue. The choice of pair may be entirely subjective, as management differ in their trade-offs across the variables. For management who are intent on lowering costs, there may be a trade-off between labour (L) and capital expenditure (K) with a shift between less labour-intensive and more capital-intensive production technology — provided productivity does not change. In such a scenario, productivity takes the place of utility — a third parameter that does not change as management decide between the pairs of less L more K, and more L less K. The difficulty lies in identifying that elusive third variable, a difficulty compounded by the subjective nature of the indifference analysis. In the Marris model, however, we identify value — market capitalisation of a company — as a candidate for the third variable that is underpinned by growth.

Opportunity Cost: Our Binary Reach

One of the key concepts in understanding the motivation of individuals is the **trade-off** or indifference embedded in a binary choice. To do X or Y, a choice must be made and it involves a trade-off. Hence, doing X incurs an opportunity cost of not doing Y.

Some of you reading this book are embarking on an MBA and will spend time in a classroom setting away from family, friends and clients. Imagine it is a balmy, warm afternoon when a casual observer sees you in a classroom rather than outside enjoying the sun. You have traded being outdoors in the sun for being indoors in class. In order for the observer to rationalise what it is he observes, he would require information on your third variable, Z, to explain the observation as a trade-off between Y (being outdoors in the sun) and X (being indoors attending a class). The objective is to maximise the value of your third variable.

Alternatively, ask yourself why your cat is not likely to stick its paw in the pool. It will not get wet because it figures that it is not worth the effort needed to dry and clean itself with its tongue to enjoy something as superficial as marine life. Unless you starve your cat and stock your pool with fish, your cat is likely to remain on dry land.

In the first example of attending a class, effort such as scheduling class attendance or investing in online teaching software will be expended to minimise the opportunity cost. Likewise, in the second example of taking a dip in the pool, effort will be expended and costs incurred in stocking the pool with fish.

Z or Third Variable

In trying to identify a third variable, type becomes important in understanding management behaviour as it can be signalled to competitors through observing their behaviour. Individuals keep to type and create patterns in their behaviour. It is these patterns of observed behaviour that companies should look for in the management of a competitor. For example, if a new CEO has a history of growing companies through acquisition, there is a high probability that the latter will keep to type in the new company and attempt to grow through acquisition than by achieving organic growth.

Detecting the identity of the third variable, Z, is interesting. Remember that management are prepared to trade off Y and X only if the value of Z, U(Z), does not change. What, then, is Z? This is a guessing game between management and the investment community, shareholders and external stakeholders, including competitors. The identity of Z could provide an insight into the strategic thinking of the management, and that becomes critical in the playing of games. Figure 1.1 illustrates a managerial indifference trade-off relationship.

Often, Z is defined as market share, growth, value or costs, but generally it is camouflaged. Management do provide signals to the market, or investment commentators and analysts contribute to the guessing game by offering opinions on the identity of Z. In the Marris model, managerial discretionary behaviour is allowed in the principal-agent

Figure 1.1
Management Indifference

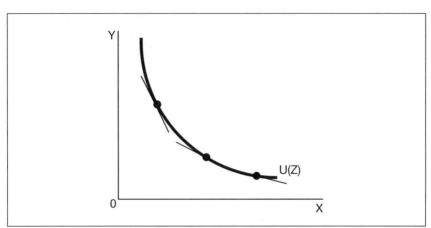

relationship. It facilitates growth. Management, therefore, have the discretion to focus on Z. By adjusting Z, management can also achieve their personal goals, such as status, power and pay.

Premium on Type

We can ascribe an indifference relationship to management type. The explanatory power of a managerial indifference relationship is greatly enhanced when we include forms of personal and social capital in the management utility function, U(Z). Management receive share options, and the share price of a company includes a premium on the type of CEO. In the case of Apple Inc, for example, there was a premium on Steve Jobs as CEO built into the share price. Management have objectives, and they derive a sense of personal satisfaction from realising those objectives. An important attribute is that type displays signals to the market, which includes consumers and competitors. More important, the signals are observed by shareholders and investors in the company. There are two important signals:

(1) dividends signal and Marris type of player, and
(2) price signal and Baumol type of player.

What does this mean? Traditionally, when company A lowers its price, it is to boost demand. The very act of lowering price may be construed by a competitor as a threat to their sales, thus provoking a price reaction. One must remember that 50p is cheap if the competitor is 60p; but reducing one's price to 30p will secure more sales only if the competitor is still 60p. The anticipation of a competitor's reaction is the essence of price signalling.

Positive Learning Transfer

In our observations, there are different time periods: t corresponds to now, and the future is represented by time period t+1. Decisions taken in time period t have consequences in time period t+1. In other words, a trade-off between two variables in time period t could be explained by the likely impact of that trade-off on a third variable in time period t+1. Consider the following scenario. Growth in a company depends upon growth in the market. In the market, the company sells a range of products. Hence, growth in the products will grow the market. Product diversification at time period t enables the company to grow organically in t+1. However, this requires investment in R&D, and technology to ensure that the products are differentiated in the market to sustain the growth in sales required to filter back into company growth.

With higher investment in R&D, there may be a claim on the finances of the company in time period t as shareholders require dividends; as more is expended on R&D, the company may approach the external market to borrow funds. Alternatively, management may decide to use internal funds to finance the R&D in period t, postpone dividend payments until period t+1 and focus on maximising the growth of the company. As the company grows and management opt to deliver dividends in period t+1, the value of the company may increase. This implicit trade-off observed in a Marris type — between payment of dividends *versus* more expenditure on R&D — is at the heart of the Marris model. The elusive third variable is the value of the company, Marris V.

How can an optimal trade-off be achieved? It can be achieved through a positive learning transfer (PLT) from the management to the shareholders by providing information and reassurance in the activities of management. Of course, if in the past management have been observed as successfully maximising growth, shareholders may be persuaded to trust the management type. However, shareholders are prone to follow a Bayesian-type rule in seeing what they want to see; if profits fall in time period t during the refocus of strategy towards more product diversification, shareholders will only see the falling profits and react by selling stock. Therefore, it is imperative for management to transfer a positive learning about their behaviour and plans to the shareholders. This can explain the willingness of many CEOs to appear on business channels such as cnbc.com, Bloomberg.com or Thomson Reuters.

Behavioural Approach

One of the more interesting applications in the business world is the use of game theory in shaping strategy. Game theory focuses on observed behaviour and allows us to identify patterns and to predict a likely future outcome. Look around you and observe the number of right-handed people you encounter. It is relatively easy to predict that if you were to hand anybody a pen, they would write with their right hand. However, if the individuals know that you are observing them as right-handed individuals, some of them may try to fool you and write using their left hands. A game of poker is a typical game of observation and trust where a sequence of moves is played, the game ends and the winnings or pay-offs are realised. The sequence of poker hands can be regarded as moves, and they represent a game. Schooled players look for connections between poker hands, and observe what every other player does or does not do as the game unfolds. Everyday in the business world, management observe rival prices, costs and share price movements. The business environment is one that is rich with observed data.

The management models depicted in Table 1.2 recognise and promote the importance of profit maximisation. Each model can be defined within the principal (shareholder)-agent (management) framework. This would imply that focusing on a single overriding goal is unrealistic. The behavioural approach recognises the multiplicity of goals

Table 1.2
Model Objectives

	Behavioural	Baumol	Marris	Framework T/3
Objective	Multiple goals	Sales	Growth	Z or third variable
Approach	Satisficing — subject to profit constraint	Maximisation — subject to profit constraint	Maximisation — subject to security constraint	Maximisation — subject to external constraints
Principal-agent relationship	Yes	Yes	Yes	Yes
Short term vs long term	Varies	Short	Long	Time period t+1
Reaction and interaction	Yes	Partial	Yes	Nash replies
Decision-making coalitions	Yes	No	No	Decision quantums

from these managerial models and allows for the greater complexity that results from moving away from a single 'maximised' result to a 'satisficed' result. It is the means by which an outcome is reached — not the goal — that is important because the outcome is a compromise on many different goals, with the influence and importance of each varying from one business to another.

Therefore, management display certain characteristics — a type — depending on their business and industry experience, costs and constraints on competition. Over time, management's objective is to increase the relative performance of the company, and Framework T/3 conceptually integrates the core of economic reasoning with the other business disciplines — such as finance and marketing — by providing a common framework for investigating and understanding management behaviour as a signalling game. Management behaviour expands with the market-as-a-game or disappears as a function of the game. In the real world, business decisions may be influenced by many different considerations. The owners and managers of firms may have various goals and objectives, especially over longer periods of time. They may conceivably be motivated by a desire to become well respected in the community, to serve some other higher purpose such as promoting their home country's national objectives or they may simply want their organisation to become as large and powerful as possible. However, the basic economic theory of business behaviour is based on a very different premise: firms exist to earn profits and the goal of management is to maximise those profits (or minimise their losses) in time period $t+1$.

Framework T/3 places emphasis on explaining decisions that are taken within the firm. In our earlier reference to the Baumol hypothesis, if management opt for a price reduction to increase total revenue, the objective will depend on the price reaction of the competitor. Thus, management type, player type and different choice situations call for different decision approaches by management. Completely rational decision making involves identifying alternatives, projecting the probabilities and outcomes of alternatives and evaluating the outcomes according to known preferences. These information-gathering and information-processing requirements are beyond the capabilities of any organisation. In practice, organisational decision making departs from the rational ideal in important ways depending on the contingencies of the decision context. Cyert and March (1963) coupled bounded rationality with the assumption that human actors are myopic, that is, they make short-term decisions.

Therefore, the behaviour of management is critically assessed in the context of testing their ability to affect outcomes. Management is to be understood in terms of a rational individual making a decision. Within the decision-making process of a modern organisation, management teams take actions according to how their combined effort and expertise impact on knowing when and how to act. The conflict —

that is, the trade-off — referred to earlier is necessarily a conflict of subjective outcomes, as different management have different outcomes with a given action.

An Evolving Process

Management A, for example, change price to achieve a subjective outcome; however, management B's reaction to the price change will depend on B's subjective outcome. Neither of them takes price as exogenous. Price is now a signal. Therefore, both A and B need to know the types of all participants in the market as well as their production technology in order to compete. The objective is to obtain a sustainable competitive advantage at $t+1$.

The price signals, for example, generate wave functions in an evolving process of actions and reactions. The author is researching this approach. Baumol type players can differ in their subjective preferences over outcomes of the game G, if playing recurrently. They reduce price, but no rival follows. Consequently, their preferences (to reduce price) can determine what is observed in the game (no one follows) and the consequent pay-offs from the game. Therefore, it is imperative for management to understand their opponent's type and their own type as perceived by their opponents. To optimise its actions, each player must understand the competitor's type in order to predict the actions of the other players in the market-as-a-game.

In Chapter 10, we advance the idea that management could consider the market as a **market system** that evolves as a sequence of moves in a game or across different games in a time continuum (Marschak and Radner, 1972). Each game, G, re-opens over time; at each move, players act so that plans for action — the market strategy — available in $t+1$ significantly affect actions at time period t.

A player's actions are restricted by an understanding of competitor type, technology in the game and time. The transaction costs of playing a game include management time and technology costs. Due to the transaction costs involved, an equilibrium may not be forthcoming early in a game. It is not transaction costs *per se* that are prohibitive, but costs arising from the sequence of boundary constraints including: (a) the likely transfer of market share and power; (b) prediction about competitors' action; and (c) identification of the near-rival — that competitor in the sum of competitors — who will react first to your move.

As an adviser, the strategist should construct a historic CTL to define a likely pattern, focus on the observed behaviour in a pattern, observe the signals and focus on the existence of a stable equilibrium in a game. This represents a long-term vision, rather than a focus on drastic changes or technology shocks, that best describes a game. Management need to understand strategy as a moving target in a time continuum; we address this later in the discussion of spherical competitors.

In the following chapters, hypotheses — based on well-defined economic models — are advanced in the search for signals. Prices, for example, are interpreted as signals in a Baumol hypothesis and price signalling is identified as a way to execute strategy. At another level, price defines the relationship with the consumer — the demand function. Dividends are introduced as a financial signal in a Marris hypothesis, signalling the use of retained profits for reinvestment, innovation and R&D. More dividend payments translate into a signal on less funds for reinvestment. This trade-off, not dissimilar to the retention ratio, defines the relationship with the investor.

In Chapter 5, capacity is presented as a signal in the production relationship. It opens a window into the ability and capability of the supply chain to produce the product and provide services at a lower unit cost of production. Capacity signalling allows us to develop a cost-leader (CL) hypothesis where players camouflage their capacity in a game. Throughout the book, key decisions on whether to compete or cooperate, to follow or lead and to enter a market translate into signals and patterns.

CHAPTER 2

Game Embedded Strategy

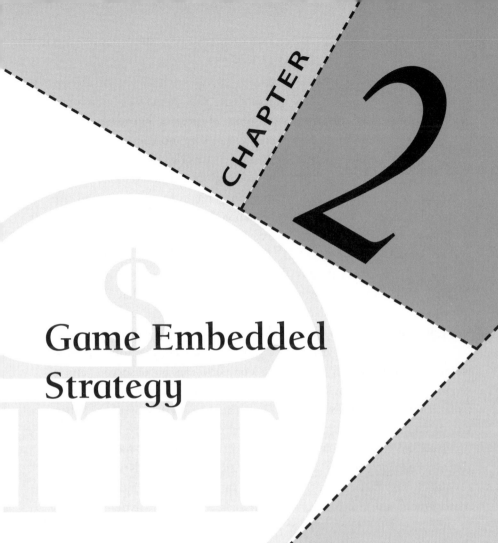

We are capable of continuing to believe things that all the evidence shows not to be true, even long after everyone has demonstrated that they're not true.—**George Orwell**

he neoclassical theory of the firm was developed based on the assumption of perfect knowledge. That assumption has been substantially modified to allow the development of sophisticated theories of decision making under conditions of uncertainty (Koutsoyiannis, 1980). Uncertainty in action arises when management have a type and are bounded rational; that is, they do not have the information that traditional theory assumes they have. As players in a game, their actions are constrained or bounded by information that may be flawed or outdated. Each player learns from other players' actions, but needs to analyse an *if-then* hypothesis in order to extract that additional information which may have led to the other players' actions. Their strategies are defined as game embedded strategies (GEM*s*).

In addition, the market is a game as rival competitors compete for market share. Each move by a company can be observed, and a sequence of moves constitutes a strategy. Type is linked to behaviour (refer to our earlier example of Leo the Liar in Chapter 1). When type is applied to management in a game of strategy, there is a need to focus on the role of subjective value and methodological individualism, that is, management as individuals realising their wills despite the resistance of others. In other words, the CEO is an individual and management are individuals; as individuals, they have a type. In trying to understand the behaviour of rational action (Jones, 2004; Mahoney, 2005; Hagstrom, 2005), views on type and related topics have deep historical roots across many disciplines.

Companies are players in a game, and the game dimensions are defined in terms of geography and product. Thus, we have some interesting observations: Google entering the US market in smartphones, Lenovo entering the market for smartphones or Apple evolving as a telecommunications player. Each observation is defined in terms of the geography and product in which the game will be played. The observations are transferred to a critical timeline that allows the observer to find a pattern in the observed points. The game begins upon the action of one player — observed as a price decrease. A second player reacts in a match-match sequence of price movements over a time period. The strategy question is framed in terms of two related issues: What did the player who initiated the price decrease believe about the likely reaction from the competitor? How long will both players, observed in a sequence of matching price moves, continue to match each other's price movements? The first question speaks to the belief system of each player; the second speaks to the concept of a Nash equilibrium.

Critical Timeline

The key to understanding management type in Framework T/3 is to understand behaviour, and to infer from observed behaviour the likely actions and reactions of management in the business world. Management can suffer from a failure to understand competitor behaviour. Part of the explanation in Chapter 1 is that management are bounded rational; they do not factor in all the possible scenarios, nor do they put in the time and effort to analyse rival behaviour. Instead, they cling on to a bunker silo approach. At the root of this failure is a misunderstanding of the importance of type. If management's decision to do X is in any way influenced by the type of rival management, competitors then do have an implicit belief system, thinking or believing what the other may do or act.

It is one thing to believe or think about how another individual is more likely to behave; in the absence of any signals, chat or communication, one must rely on one's belief system. Alternatively, management can observe behaviour as signals and discover the patterns. The pattern can be difficult to determine and requires many years of observations. In the interim, we can read the signals of CEO type by listening to their views on cnbc.com or Bloomberg.com, conferences or company briefings to the equity markets. Each CEO has a type, a particular economic characteristic that gives a clue to strategy. It is imperative to observe signals in order to understand type. Patterns do emerge in the observed behaviour, price movements or growth through acquisition. The patterns create a critical timeline (CTL) of observed actions; as the CTL unfolds, it reveals a strategy. In his book, McNutt (2008) discusses the CTL for Microsoft and Sony during the period 2000 to 2004 with the launch of PS2 and Xbox. A comparison of the CTLs for Nissan and General Motors can help to evaluate the strategy adopted at Nissan (Figure 2.1). Likewise, refer to the CTL for Apple and Nokia in Figure 7.3 on page 112, when Nokia competed against Apple in digital music services during the period 2005 to 2008.

Pattern Recognition

It is a good mental exercise to try to translate actions and reactions into a pattern, and to observe how a defined pattern builds up, is repeated and becomes predictable. The selection of CTLs in the Appendix at the end of the book illustrates the scope and range of patterns across different markets. The key to successful strategic planning is successful strategic thinking. To do CTL analysis, a company should ask itself five questions and reflect on the answers:

(1)   What market should I be in?
(2)   Who is my near-rival?
(3)   What is the near-rival's type?
(4)   Are my actions being observed?
(5)   What is my type as a player?

Game embedded strategies (GEMs) provide an innovative approach to our understanding of the economics of strategy. The focus is very much on the individual firm — the individual decision-maker — rather than on an industry *per se*. Companies are complex organisations, but the actions and reactions of companies are made up of small things. For instance, a key executive decides to launch a new product, a team develops an entry plan for a new geographic market or a regional pricing manager opts to change price. Each decision is an action, and each action is a signal. Signals convey meaning about type and players tend to believe what is observed, as long as such belief is consistent with rationality and the incentives in the game.

Observe, Not Judge

The primary interest in GEMs is the pattern of behaviour represented by signals in the play of a game. Economic theory allows us to

Figure 2.1
Critical Timeline — Nissan *vs* General Motors

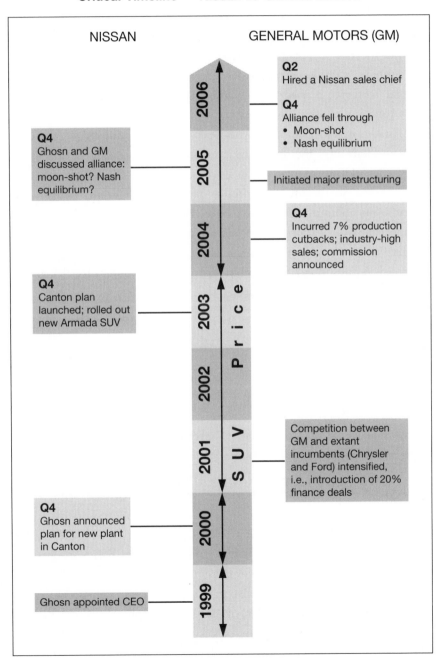

calculate actions and reactions, but strategists are interested in calculating the probability that a particular action will lead to a reaction in
time. The objective of the strategist is to not only define competition
and rival behaviour, but also to widen the definition of competition.
To imagine how a specific reaction will occur at a particular time is
the strategist's challenge, as presented in this book. Numbers do follow
Fermat patterns; if share prices and product prices are numbers, they
must follow a pattern (unobserved).

In the efficient market hypothesis, available knowledge is already
incorporated into the price of securities such as shares, bonds or
currencies. However, the knowledge may neither be accurately nor
completely incorporated as individuals have different beliefs and
perceptions about an uncertain future. Patterns take away the cobwebs
of uncertainty and afford strategists the opportunity to extract the value
of the information contained in a pattern of action and reaction. The
approach as described falls within the genre of observational learning
— we observe, but do not judge.

Zero-sum Constraint

In the competitive environment known as oligopoly where there are
five or fewer rival competitors, a degree of interdependence arises in
the market. Interdependence creates a game dimension and transforms management into players. Therefore, it behoves us to look at
both management type and player type, reserving the latter term to
describe the behaviour of firms and companies as we have come to
understand them in modern business. In the case of Intel *versus* AMD
in microprocessors, the gain in market share by one competitor is at
the expense of the other as they try to increase or consolidate market
share. In many markets, a unilateral gain in market share can occur as
a direct consequence of a loss accruing to a competitor.

The zero-sum constraint also acts as an external constraint. When
management realise that their pricing and output decisions depend
as much on the likely reactions of competitors as they do on understanding their consumers, they may have to understand that there is a

price and quantity output that is the best they can achieve given the likely reactions of their competitors. It is not, however, the best they can achieve in terms of their own motives. This is the Nash premise (see Figure 2.2) which we will discuss in a later chapter.

Figure 2.2
Nash Premise

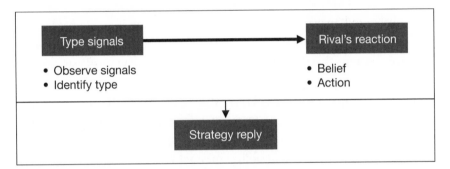

The zero-sum constraint can easily arise in product markets where there are fickle preferences and changing demand for increasingly differentiated products amongst consumers. A player can lag behind in the market due to an inability to differentiate fast enough. This is contrary to the Model-T effect: consumers will buy a Model-T — available only in the colour black — but over time, preferences will change and more consumers will buy different brands of coloured cars. Growth and discretionary theories — such as Marris and Baumol — start from the same point that management have power over an objective function. Included in a managerial objective function are the motives of management: a desire for sustainable long-term growth in the size of the company as measured by (say) assets, employees, output or market share. In managerial theories, the pursuit of managerial motives is subject to external shareholder constraint. The motives of management reveal their type.

Penrose Effect

The real-world competitive environment is different from the textbook model of the perfectly competitive economy. In a perfectly competitive market, product markets are assumed to be supplied by a large number of small single-plant, single-product and owner-managed price-taking firms with limited, if any, capacity for growth. Economists began responding to this from the mid-1950s to the mid-1970s, and their responses can be classified into three distinct groups: discretionary theories (Baumol, 1959; Williamson, 1971), growth-oriented theories (Penrose, 1959; Marris, 1964; Mueller, 1972) and bureaucratic theories (Monsen and Downs, 1965). Today, in the 21st century, the focus is on the behavioural analysis of business decision making.

The modern company is a bureaucratic structure with an administrative system that could frustrate the achievement of sustainable growth. Consequently, there are unique internal constraints in each company. The management operate within this structure; problems may arise within the management team on information about opportunities for growth, or top management may not be capable of making a decision. In other words, management ability may act as a constraint on achieving a growth rate through time. This is referred to as the **Penrose effect**, and it represents a tangible cost of growth in the company. It is the failure to understand rival type and its implications that exacerbates the Penrose effect. It is imperative for management to realise that their respective actions are interdependent. Once management recognise their interdependence and act accordingly, they are in what we label a game dimension. How to incorporate the rival's type into the decision on X will be guided by the rules of sequential non-cooperative games; how best to respond will ultimately depend on the underlying cost and production technology of the company as a player in a game.

Trust

In the game, building trust is an important rule. It is central to the Prisoners' Dilemma (PD). It is critical for management to understand the dilemma in order to avoid incurring a Penrose effect. In the original PD, two prisoners are faced with a dilemma when caught by the police for burglaries: Do they trust each other enough to cooperate to minimise total loss of liberty or will one of them — trusting the other to cooperate — betray her so as to go free? Knowing that there is a bond of trust, the police interview each prisoner separately and tell each of them that the other has informed on her. Does each prisoner trust her friend, or does she betray the friend and take the deal from the police? Both prisoners betray in the absence of a strong bond of trust. The strategy of betrayal or confession is defined as a dominant strategy — the best (or worst) — regardless of how the rival plays.

The winnings or pay-offs are determined by the components of the market-as-a-game. The game occurs when an action leads to a reaction. It is a measure of strategic advantage if management have anticipated the likely reaction and are not surprised by it. The key parameters in this game include rival management type, which can be observed by signals from senior management (see Table 2.1). It is equally important to deduce how one's type is perceived by competitors in the market-as-a-game.

In general, the application of game theory to management and business is very important, particularly in a zero-sum market where two or three firms collectively have 100 per cent of the market share (Nalebuff and Dixit, 2008; Baye, 2008). This is the classic oligopoly market structure, in which the players recognise their mutual independence. A strategy set is a sequence of moves. A sequence could be composed of a move either to cooperate or to compete. Competition policy and antitrust rules exist in many jurisdictions to dissuade firms from forming a credible cartel arrangement. Cartels are inherently unstable because of an incentive to cheat. Modern companies do compete by cooperating through joint ventures, technology sharing and outsourcing. In an oligopoly market with five players, the presence of an acute zero-

Table 2.1
Typology on Type

Signal	Type	Observation
Price	Baumol	Low prices
Dividends	Marris	R&D increase
Costs	Cost leadership	Reduce costs

sum constraint and interdependence can trigger off a merger wave in the industry. In other words, when management realise that they are players and the market shapes the dimension of the game, an alternative to competing is simply to cooperate or merge. Nonetheless, there is always the element of trust.

If the players trust each other, they believe the signals in the market. However, there is still a preference for dishonesty amongst some players. Therefore, it is critical to understand the type of player in the game. Chandler's (1962) thesis is that structure follows strategy; it is the behaviour of management — observed in the CTL as strategy by competitors — that determines the market structure. If a firm's strategy is to be carried out or implemented, individuals working in the firm must know the strategy and its operational requirements for tasks and actions. As players, how management respond to problems of information, innovation, coordination and commitment in a game will determine the long-term position of the company.

What Market Should We Be In?

It is critical for management to answer the question "What market should we be in?" (see Figure 2.3). A company should not be in a market-as-a-game unless they understand the dimensions of the game, that is, the number of players and their type.

Figure 2.3
Game Embedded Strategy

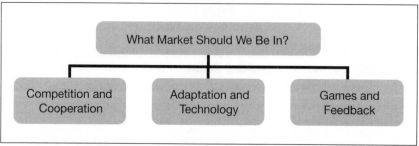

The decision-making process in GEMs involves a choice between three possible scenarios:

(1) competition and cooperation,
(2) adaptation and
(3) technology, game and feedback.

It is difficult to determine what market the company should be in as this varies from one firm to another depending on the influence that individual management is able to exercise on management type and player type, and on how responsive shareholders are to adjusting management expectations. The outcome will also be influenced by the decision-making process *per se* in the firm and a willingness to follow the rules. When management discount the likely reaction of a competitor to an impending price change, they are said to be in a 'game' where decisions and outcomes are interdependent. The degree of interdependence is important: as the number of competitors falls below five (oligopoly), there is a mutual understanding — driven by the innate structure of the market — that each company in an oligopoly structure could do better in the absence of price competition. It is a different matter to announce that management proceed to cooperate; on the contrary, we begin from the premise of non-cooperation.

In a GEMs environment of non-cooperation with mutual inter-dependence, a decision by company A will lead to a reaction from company B. Therefore, A should expect a reaction from B and *vice versa*. If the management of company A have no contingency in terms of a reaction from B, there is the possibility of misguided decision making by A. The expectation of a likely reaction and its computation is at the heart of the economics of strategy. The strategy emphasises the use of non-cooperative game theory as a tool of analysis to understand management behaviour. Careful attention is given to management type and the identification of signals from the decisions, actions and commentary of management. Decisions on price and costs, for example, are taken in the context of likely reactions from competitors.

Camouflage + Surprise = Ambush Strategy

In *Jungle Warfare*, John Cross (1989) provides an interesting discussion of military ambush strategy during World War II. According to Cross, ambushes can be of any shape, but basically they are linear and cover a geographical area. The CTL is a linear concept and allows management to identify a pattern of observed behaviour based on a wheel of belief as illustrated in Figure 2.4. The geography and the product spaces define the dimensions of the game. The author continues to identify the parameters for success: "For success, a few things not to be forgotten on the battlefield: surprise, silence, security, a rehearsal whenever possible and a reserve" (page 211). Earlier in the book, he argues that an adverse reaction on being surprised can be minimised by well-tried and instinctive immediate action drills. Nonetheless, there are signals, as indicated in this passage on tracking discipline:

Figure 2.4
The Wheel of Belief

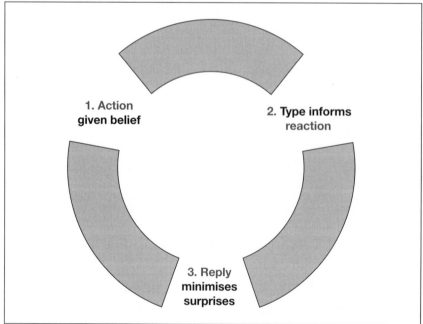

1. Action given belief

2. Type informs reaction

3. Reply minimises surprises

"One successful alternative was leaving the track walking backwards into the jungle with some of the force continuing walking forwards then leaving the track into the jungle on the opposite side … [sic]; this was risky as the footprint of those walking backwards (when the toe imprint is greater) and those walking forwards (when the heel imprint is greater) are patently obvious" (page 87). The linearity is captured by the CTL which tracks a range of observations, including price and product specifications.

The area dimension of ambush strategy is about geography. In late 2008, a company in China called Tencent emerged as a leading player in the instant text messaging (IM) market ahead of MSN. Tencent's success was linked to the demand for IM from young, newly employed Chinese consumers. The threat from the new third-generation cellular networks offering more Chinese consumers access to mobile email will appear on the horizon in 2009 to 2010 as they begin to roll out their services. How should Tencent react? One possibility is to adopt a 'well-tried and instinctive immediate action drill'. Tencent's success is based on the social networking and online gaming services it provides. Hence, T/3 would recommend that Tencent 'walks forward' with a strategy to build on these two aspects of ambush strategy by introducing a range of functionalities that are better (camouflage) than those currently available on tried and tested networks abroad (surprise).

What-if, If-then

Today, Tencent is China's largest online player. By learning how much its consumers can be enticed to use its new products and services such as WeChat (which will be launched in mid-2013), the information and knowledge gleaned can be used to inform Tencent's management on their pricing and revenue policy.

However, as a player in a game, Tencent's management must find the main battlefield to concentrate their fighting power in a game of camouflage and surprise. In other words, management need to ask two important questions: Who is our near-rival? Who, amongst the sum of competitors, is more likely to react first?

Tencent's IM service is competing against China Mobile, the dominant mobile player in mainland China. Analysts believe that China Mobile's total revenue is reliant on the revenue stream from text messaging. Tencent has signalled its plans to grow revenues in $t+1$ by introducing games aimed at mobile users. **What if** its WeChat strategy provokes a reaction not only from China Mobile, but also from Weibo-Alibaba?

By unravelling patterns in the historic reactions of its competitors, Tencent's management will find the answer to its first question: Who is our near-rival? Let us hypothesise as follows: **If** Tencent's near-rival in $t+1$ is likely to be Weibo-Alibaba, **then** the game dimension is likely to be in messaging and mobile games in China and in Asia. With this information, Tencent can 'walk forward' into the main battlefield in 2013 and 2014 with a CTL of connected patterns and a strategy reply as outlined in Figure 2.2.

CHAPTER 3

Baumol Hypothesis

*Ah, but I was so much older then,
I'm younger than that now.*
—**Bob Dylan**

I n the history of economics applied to the business world, many scholars and practitioners were sceptical about the focus on managerial behaviour. During the latter half of the 20th century, managerial theories of the firm began to emerge in the literature as economic theories on how the behaviour of modern management affected the working of the economic system, rather than the other way around. The debate on strategy determining structure is implicit in the Chicago hypothesis of modern antitrust, and the **Chandler dilemma** is a key component of strategic management. They have, however, been the subject of considerable research in the management literature.

This book is not about the models *per se*; however, some of the managerial models will inform our discussion of type (see Table 2.1 on page 33). As suggested, Baumol type is related to the fundamentals of the Baumol model: there is a correlation between price and total revenue, depending on the price elasticity of demand. When a price reduction is observed, rival management should stop and think: Is it a one-shot price reduction to increase total revenue? How rival management respond depends on their belief system and what they observe as signals in the market.

Hence, type is ascribed to management as a unique — and sometimes idiosyncratic — behavioural characteristic that can be inferred from understanding the motives of management. Arguably, management in debates over strategy can look to behavioural theories about type to gain a better appreciation of the assumptions and foundations of their own business acumen. For type to be relevant to an understanding of modern business, we will argue throughout that outcomes — as measured by key financial indicators — are equally likely across management, but information about a competitor's management type delivers a competitive advantage.

Oligopoly n < 5

Five is the key number of competitors (n) in a market. With five or fewer competitors, each competitor becomes increasingly aware of the degree of mutual interdependence within the group. Framework T/3 could provide management with a framework to assess the competitive environment in markets that are increasingly being defined by a smaller number of competing firms. How small? Increasingly, markets are characterised by five or fewer rival competitors — the quintessential oligopoly market structure. In everyday experience, management as a team are concerned with price and quantity outcomes in an oligopoly market, as well as how those outcomes could change from one particular circumstance to another in that competitive environment. For example, the appointment of a new CEO by a rival could change the outcomes and dimensions of the game.

In the literature, dissatisfaction with the simple concept of a firm as a mechanism that transforms atomistic inputs into marketable outputs has resulted in alternative perspectives of the firm. There is a new emphasis on the internal structure of the corporate firm, and the emerging managerial theory stresses the complex nature of the modern corporate firm (Brickley, 2007). In their pioneering work, Berle and Means (1932) describe the diminishing influence of shareholders in the decision-making process of large corporations in the United States at the turn of the 20th century. This left much of the decision making to management whose objectives could be different from those of the owners of the firm. If, in terms of its influence on managers' salaries, size of firm was — for example — more important than firms' profitability, growth could be a more important objective of firms than profit. This is the key to unlocking the third variable.

Other reasons were advanced as to why management may be more preoccupied with sales or revenue maximisation than with profit maximisation (Baumol, 1967). If sales fail to rise, this is often equated with reduced market share and market power and, consequently, with increased vulnerability to the actions of competitors. Under a zero-sum constraint, management may not realise their sales targets as rivals poach market share. When asked about the way his company performs, an executive would typically reply in terms of what the firm's levels of sales are. The financial market and retail distributors are more responsive to a firm with rising sales. The model developed by Baumol attempts to reconcile the behavioural conflict between profit maximisation and maximisation of the firm's sales, its total revenue. It assumes that the firm maximises sales revenue subject to a minimum profit constraint.

Elasticity

The revenue-maximising level of output is the level at which the marginal revenue is 0 and the elasticity of demand is 1. For a Baumol total revenue sales maximising firm, prices are low when demand is elastic; that is, for every 10 per cent reduction in price, total revenue would increase by at least 10 per cent. Embedded in the demand relationship is a measurement of how responsive demand is to price changes. This is called price elasticity, ϵ_p. It is a key link between price and total revenue. A supplier will supply more if the price increases, subject to production constraints. However, at the higher price with greater supply, a key question remains: Is the total revenue accruing from the additional supply higher than before the price change? This goes to the heart of the concept of elasticity, which measures the responsiveness of demand to price:

$$\epsilon_p = \frac{\%\Delta q}{\%\Delta p}$$

Remember that the formula for total revenue (TR) is TR $=$ p.q. Therefore, any change in TR can come about from either a price change, $\%\Delta p$, or a change in demand (at a given price), $\%\Delta q$.

The q is the amount of product purchased by the rational consumer. For some products, if the price increases, TR will increase. There are products for which TR will increase only if the price falls. The former are inelastic products and the latter are elastic products. The key driver is the responsiveness of demand to price changes. This is clearly illustrated later in the chapter.

Baumol Type

A Baumol type focuses on pricing as a driver of revenue and volumes, but may face a cost-volume constraint. Market share is the Z variable and lower profit margins are in a trade-off with higher volumes. Competitors would observe a Baumol-type strategy based on leveraging revenues from a pricing policy. Provided demand is sufficiently elastic, a price reduction should produce the increase in intended sales revenue. It is by reducing price that management are able to maximise revenue yield from the asset. This is known in the industry as yield per passenger, average revenue per user (ARPU) or breakeven price, as illustrated by the revenue curve at Point A in Figure 3.1 where total cost equals total revenue.

The business model works until elasticity falls: initially, elasticity is high as consumers switch from good or service X to the Baumol good or service Y. However, the preference set of the once-X-now-Y consumers changes as they experience the good, but with lower opportunity costs. These are known as switching costs. To understand this, recall that the revenue is TR = p.q and that ΔTR = Δp.q is to be followed by Δq at the new lower p, Δp. There is a sequence in pricing as revenue awaits the lag in quantity-sales response. For various reasons, particularly to do with quality and price, consumers may be weary of a price reduction from the higher priced elastic segment. In that segment, the higher prices have been sustained and supported probably by increased advertising and consumer persuasion. Or the Δq may not materialise as consumers remain loyal to a rival player. Even with Δp = 8, the final lower price may still be higher relative to a rival's price. Hence, Baumol pricing —

Figure 3.1
Baumol Model and Breakeven Price

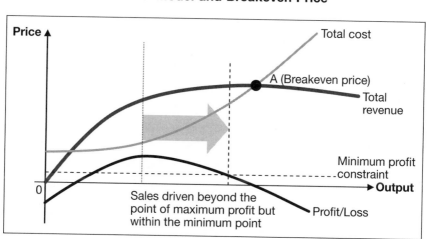

Table 3.1
Total Revenue Test

	Price increase	Price decrease
ϵp > 1: Elastic	TR decreases	TR increases
ϵp < 1: Inelastic	TR increases	TR decreases

favoured by the low-cost airlines' model of revenue yield management — would fit into the top right-hand corner of Table 3.1.

Paradox of Tumbling Price

There is a trigger price, at which point elasticity changes from an elastic range above the trigger price to an inelastic range below the trigger price (see Figure 3.2). At the trigger price, ϵp = 1. It is significant because it determines the total revenue response to any price change.

Figure 3.2
Trigger Price

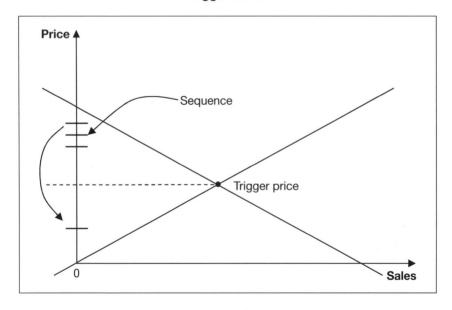

Consider the following example. If the current price is 40p and a trigger price is computer-generated at 31p, it will be strategic for management not to proceed with a 10p reduction in price because at 30p, the reduced price is less than the trigger price: 30p < 31p. Instead, a price reduction of less than 9p (no more than 8p) would fall within the trigger price boundary constraint; as price falls from 40p to 32p, revenue should increase under the total revenue test.

The trigger price can complement the mark-up price P > AVC and the net margin price P > AC, where AVC is the average variable cost and AC is the total average cost (as discussed in Chapter 5).

Sales Fuel Profits

The paradox of the tumbling price described in Chapter 1 can be overcome with price positioning by using different prices at different times for different consumers. The paradox adds to the complexity of what price to charge by raising the issue of how much the reduction or increase in price should be. That belies the fact that management would always wish to reduce price outside the remit of price wars, price promotion and price discrimination.

Conversely, increasing price from a relatively lower base requires sufficient spend on advertising to ensure that that segment of the demand function complies with inelasticity. Empirical evidence has concluded that increased advertising expenditure rescues the elasticity of demand less than 1, but this applies to the entire range and overall slope of the demand (Schmalensee, 1979).

In the segment, management should think of the low price as a penetration price strategy; once price is well below a trigger price, only then should a price increase be considered. If advertising expense is increased, the lower segment encroaches on the entire demand. In other words, an inelastic entire demand will have a greater probability of inelastic segments.

It is important for management, in general, to realise that sales revenue growth (ΔTR) — adjusted for market growth — represents market share gain. Essentially, management are creating demand as well as building a brand.

Mun and Hotelling: Price Discrimination

A strategy to achieve sales revenue growth can be found in the mercan-
tilist theories of Thomas Mun. According to Mun's strategy, a product
enters the market at a lower price, market share is cultivated and *only*
then should price increase, thereby ensuring a small but insignificant
drop in sales revenue. This strategy is better known in marketing as
'penetration pricing'. If a trigger price is high because of the low level of
elasticity, management should consider positioning the product's price
at the higher end of the price scale and, in effect, be dissuaded from
reducing price. In the latter case, even with the poaching of market
share by generic products, branded products should distance their
prices as far away as allowed by the boundaries of the trigger price
from the relatively lower priced generic.

This line of argument accords with an interpretation of Harold
Hotelling's principle of maximal differentiation. As an intermediary
price strategy, price discrimination should be considered a deliberate,
non-price war attempt to offer consumers a range of prices for the same
product. First-degree discrimination requires arbitrage and negotiation, and is more appropriate in the pricing of services. For example,
in holding on to clients' accounts, advertising executives may engage
in this form of pricing. However, it is the second and third degrees
that should interest the discerning strategic player. With second-
degree pricing, volume discounts — as well as coupon pricing and the
'six-pack phenomenon' — are offered. Under third-degree pricing,
depending on how the market is fragmented, different prices could be
charged to different consumers at different times of the day. Ironically,
third-degree pricing allows management to pass the total revenue test,
as the relatively lower price is charged to the more elastic segment
of the market (see Table 3.2).

Each of these pricing strategies allows management to price-
position their products while taking cognisance of the boundaries of the
trigger price. Price As a signal, price impacts on the magnitude of any
price change and guides the appropriateness of the price direction for a
given demand function. While recognising that demand can both shift
and change in slope, the trigger price develops a strategic angle when

Table 3.2
Price Elasticity and the Impact of Pricing Decisions Revenue

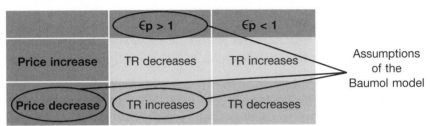

	$\epsilon p > 1$	$\epsilon p < 1$	Assumptions of the Baumol model
Price increase	TR decreases	TR increases	
Price decrease	TR increases	TR decreases	

it is complemented by the three price strategies just discussed. What is important is the relevance of elasticity to the debate. It is more than a response variable and plays a very important and strategic role in any pricing game. While the behavioural models help to instill greater realism into economic modelling, the profit constraint is still an absolute. Should the firm continue to make extremely irrational decisions, eventually the economic consequences of failing to maximise the profitability of the company will take their toll. The degree of leeway in performance would, therefore, be proportional to the size of the firm, its market share and the profit margins that it enjoys. Ultimately, it depends on management type.

Elasticity and the Want Paradox

If price is the key driver of revenues in the business model, product price elasticity of demand must be computed. Although net total revenue will increase for a product with elastic demand, as price falls there is a danger that in a product market where consumers expect more 'bells and whistles' net total revenue will fall as price falls. In short, 'bells and whistles' reduce the price elasticity of demand. This has an interesting application to the low-cost airlines' (LCA) pricing model. Initially, low prices persuade passengers to switch from rail or ship to plane. As they become more accustomed to airline travel, they expect more bells and whistles for the low price. A change in elasticity will frustrate the revenue projections in the LCA pricing model, unless:

(1) there is greater price discrimination to exploit different elasticities of demand or

(2) the geography of the market expands.

Paradoxically, as the LCA player enters new markets, the increase in player competition in the geographic market will generate an elastic (industry) demand (see Figure 3.3).

Significantly, passengers who may never have travelled by plane will be the most vociferous in demanding the bells and whistles. It is the phenomenon of the want paradox: we do not need the product called 'unknown', but once it is available we all want 'unknown' and wonder how we survived without it. The fax machine, email and mobile phones are modern examples of this phenomenon, the impact of which is to reduce price elasticity. However, the product life cycle may be short — new 'unknown' products emerge to displace existing products, such as email replacing fax — or more bells and whistles are expected, as with mobile phones where preference is as likely to be determined by

Figure 3.3
Pricing and Total Revenue Test

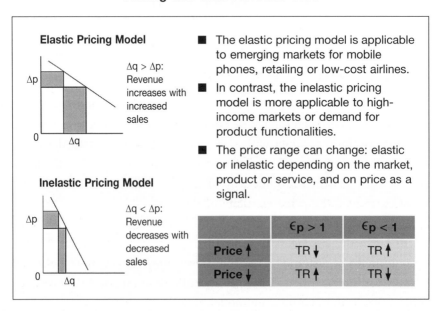

the pixel quality of the inbuilt camera, the speed of video download, gigabyte capacity for music content or some other functionality as it is by the actual price or tariff charged.

But do we — as rational consumers — buy goods? The purchase of a smartphone, for example, is about belonging to an ecosystem such as the iOs, Android or Windows 8; buying coffee is more about the coffee experience; and buying a house is more about living in a preferred neighbourhood. This means that the product is a process where you — the consumer — want X rather than the good that produces X. The consumer has time-dependent preferences. Price and income are of secondary importance in explaining demand as the rational consumer waits. It is not that an iPhone 5 is a smartphone *per se* that explains its demand, but rather it is the **process** that you — the consumer — want. Consequently, demand is inelastic and the rational consumer's real price can be defined by the zero price (0,0) equation:

$$(0,0) + \text{Opportunity Costs (Waiting Time)} = \text{Real Price}$$

When the player delays the product to market, a rational consumer waits; the more the consumer is prepared to wait, the longer the delay to market. The delay creates an inelastic demand and, on arrival, the price of the good is higher than it would otherwise be in a competitive market. The player does not carry inventory; however, you — the consumer — do incur waiting costs. In Chapter 5, we address this phenomenon as 'production driving demand' and integrate it into a strategic response from a player faced with consumers with time-dependent preferences.

Marris Hypothesis

Mark and learn, Amy. Mark and learn.
—**Charles Dickens**

I n the long term, stock investment is all about dividends; the value of a portfolio should correspond closely to the present value of dividends. If shareholders really need cash, they can sell equity. Many companies are sitting on cash and do not want to invest until they have a clear vision of the game. In low-interest environments, investors' demand for dividend-paying stocks will be strong. However, we should examine the company's fundamentals, especially if management signal that a profit warning falls below analysts' expectations. But are dividends the best way for companies to use their excess cash? Do dividends matter?

If a company pays out cash, that cash is no longer on its balance sheet. The book value of the company — its assets minus its liabilities — reduces by that amount it has paid out. Cash belongs to shareholders, be it on the balance sheet or paid out in dividend cheques. A high dividend yield, like a low price/earnings ratio, is a signal that the market is undervaluing a stock. What if dividends are a signal? A natural question that arises is whether dividend signals at different times in a game contribute equally to the equity risk premium.

Why Marris?

To answer our question, we need to understand the indifference relationship embedded in the Marris hypothesis — a downward-sloping relationship between dividend growth and R&D expenditure. An important element of the Marris hypothesis is that the portfolio of growth firms has cash flows that are more front-loaded than that of the portfolio of value firms.

Dividends are assumed to have a predictable component in financial modelling. However, the signalling of unexpected dividends growth creates a shock for *Bayesian shareholders* that may be negatively correlated with the Marris V ratio. They tend to panic and sell their equity in the belief that more dividends today signal less growth potential tomorrow. A positive learning transfer (PLT) signal translates a negative dividend shock into a higher expected growth rate in $t+1$. PLT is about reassuring shareholders that no unnecessary risks are being taken. It is about keeping 'the show on the road' during a game.

Companies need to raise capital to develop new products and invest in R&D. The market value of a company is dependent on the underlying growth potential as measured by investment in product diversification. The Marris model offers an opportunity to chart a measure of profitability defined in terms of gross profit margin and capital turnover ratio. The measure can be captured by the equation $g_d = g_c = \alpha * p$, known as the **balanced growth path** (BGP) or valuation curve. One can observe guidance on profit margins filtering into profitability as an incumbent player competes against other incumbents and new entrants. Lower than forecast margins disappoint market investors, but they also signal a degree of competition in the market. Financial markets adjust to every piece of information, and signalling quickly adjusts share prices to a fair value. Later in the chapter, we explore how BGP can be used to determine whether a company's share price at time period t is the best estimate of its true value. Part of the rationale for Framework T/3 is an attempt to find a pattern in observed behaviours and phenomena using management type and time as the two key determinants.

However, competition in the product market — which determines market share performance — can be defined in terms of T/3 under the umbrella of Francis Edgeworth's (see Chapter 1) strategic complements on price — aggressive price matching — or in terms of strategic substitutes across market shares. We address these issues later in the chapter. In the interim, suffice it to say that strategic substitutes may be captured by the zero-sum constraint where a player gains market share at the expense of a competitor. The key point here is that if capital is raised to fund growth — such as via product diversification — the expectations of consumers regarding the product's bells and whistles will constrain the growth target if the product's technology lags behind the time-dependent preferences of the consumers. If a player can sell large volumes, it should help support the profit margin. Increased competition, for example, is a significant factor behind a decline in profit margin, particularly when the player is unable to differentiate fast enough in the market.

Our focus in this chapter is the Marris model. The 1966 formulation has become "the standard one for analysis of [the growth of] the managerially controlled firm" (Hay and Morris, 1991). In his model,

Marris presented the hypothesis that managerial control would lead to growth as an objective, showing that shareholders were a less important constraint on such firms than financial markets. The Marris model is dynamic in the sense that it incorporates growth. Like Baumol's model, it assumes that management will act to maximise their utilities rather than profits; unlike Baumol, it assumes that this will be achieved through growth rather than sales.

We have selected this model because it represents one of the few explicit analyses of firm growth. Moreover, it has greater relevance today as it is imperative for management to communicate performance indicators to shareholders on a regular basis. More important, many companies today have too much cash on their books. Should they return cash to shareholders or invest it? For example, both Apple Inc and Pfizer Inc have excess cash today, but do they have the potential to invest in new products to secure long-term growth in time period $t+1$? By revisiting the mechanics of the Marris model 40 years later, we are able to present a signalling option that fits within the parameters of Framework T/3 and offers management a cash cure. The simplifying assumption of a BGP as the concave function in Figure 4.2 (see page 58) allows management to formulate a long-run equilibrium growth model. In this model, the firm's rate of demand-side growth must balance its rate of supply-side growth as the explicit factors that influence both sides are identified within T/3.

Dividends *versus* R&D Trade-off

In the literature, there is a consensus that Marris proposed a model of key metrics of firm performance, including sales growth and profitability. Sales growth depends on the success of R&D expenditure in achieving product diversification. Even so, management are faced with an interesting trade-off, as illustrated in Figure 4.1: To invest more in R&D or return cash to shareholder investors? We call this the dividends paradox. It is discussed in detail in the following pages.

Figure 4.1 shows that there is a trade-off between the proportion of profit paid out by the firm and how much it can grow; each

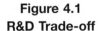

Figure 4.1
R&D Trade-off

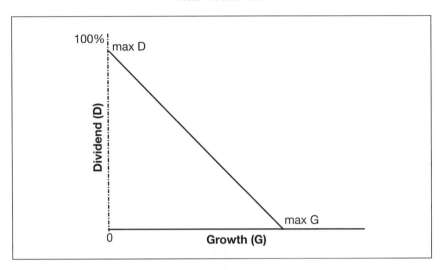

time the firm reduces the dividend proportion by moving down the vertical axis, it can finance extra growth. The key issue confronting shareholders is whether the investment being financed by paying out less in current dividends eventually produces more profits and future dividends. Shareholders have to trust management on this.

The g_d Equation: Minimal Debt

Where does a firm obtain its supply of capital (g_c)? In the finance literature, there are two sources: debt or equity. Contrary to the emerging theory at the time on the relevance of debt financing *versus* equity financing to the value of the company, Marris promoted minimal debt. Once equity capital is injected into the company, it can be used for R&D expenditure and/or returning dividends to equity investors. Hence, the demand for capital (g_d), has two sources: an internal management demand for more R&D expenditure and an external shareholder demand for more cash through dividends. There is a trade-off. The Marris trade-off can be summarised by the Koeller-Lechler equation:

$$g_d = g_c = \alpha^* p$$

The equation determines the Marris player's equilibrium growth rate and rate of return on its capital (p). According to standard accounting principles, the term p in Marris' model is influenced by the firm's capital (asset) turnover ratio measured as output/capital. This ratio is an indicator of the operating effectiveness of the firm — the extent to which the firm's asset base has been used to generate sales. Relative ineffectiveness of the firm's sales efforts would result in a lower rate of return on capital, p, and a reduced growth rate.

Furthermore, the term p is also influenced by the profit margin on sales — measured as profit/output — which can be interpreted as an indicator of the firm's operating efficiency. We can rewrite the g_d equation as follows:

$$\frac{\text{Profit}}{\text{Output}} \times \frac{\text{Output}}{\text{Capital}} = \frac{\text{Profit}}{\text{Capital}}$$

$$= \text{profitability}$$

$$= p$$

Relative inefficiency of the firm's operations (expenses increase relative to sales) would result in a lower value for p. The presence of bounded rationality, for example, or the Penrose effect — though not specified as such by Marris — could result in inward shifts of the BGP.

The firm's demand-side growth rate (g_d) is determined by the extent of product development, which is related to its goal of increasing the profit rate. The achievement of this goal depends on the firm's managerial capacity to successfully promote product development. According to Marris, demand-side product development efforts should eventually lower the firm's rate of return on capital if one assumes diminishing returns to product development activities. Improvement of the firm's managerial capacity in playing the game can be expected to moderate the demand-side trade-off between growth and profitability.

The supply-side growth rate (g_c) of the firm's capital base is dependent on the extent of internal financing from profits, where the parameter α^* reflects the maximum extent of new investment that can be financed per unit of profitability. The value of α^* is determined by shareholders' interests in avoiding low profits and possible takeover of the firm by rival competitors.

The Dividends Paradox

In the Marris model, management are faced with a trade-off between R&D expenditure and payment of dividends. Management do not wish to cease growing and, hence, retain an increasing proportion of profits in time period t to finance increased growth in time period $t+1$. What happens when growth is curtailed? For example, this could arise in some product markets where the company is unable to differentiate its products and sevices quickly enough. To sustain the market value of the company, should management pay dividends or retain more modest profits?

Scouller (2005) argues that management can enjoy fast growth while benefiting shareholders; their retained cash is being spent better than if they had invested it elsewhere. However, on account of management concern with their own security from a possible takeover by rival competitors, they would be unlikely to push their activity so far as to dilute the market value of their own shares sufficiently to create a reverse risk of their own takeover. Eventually, the new markets saturate; unless other similarly profitable markets are found, the firm becomes mature and value peaks.

Within Framework T/3, dividends are regarded as signals and the payment of dividends can influence the share price. If the dividends signal is interpreted as lack of product innovation in the g_d side of the equation, management must engage in PLT by communicating to shareholders that in time period $t+1$ value will be restored. To one investor, the share value may signal the company's ability to pay dividends; to another, payment of dividends signals an absence of R&D and innovation. Therefore, PLT is one way to ensure share prices reflect the execution of strategy.

Marris' Balanced Growth Path

In Figure 4.2, rather than at a point X where the valuation would be maximised, management choose to situate the firm at a point Y where, under certain constraints, the growth rate is maximised. Marris represented his classic trade-off outcome by plotting the profit rate p *versus* the growth rate g.

Alternatively, in Figure 4.2, we have plotted the firm's 'valuation ratio' — the name given by Marris to the ratio of market value to underlying asset value, and subsequently termed q by Tobin — and growth rate. It allows for an interesting trade-off: management may pursue a faster growth rate at the price of reducing the valuation ratio to below its maximum. Note that a robust empirical relationship between low valuation ratio and statistically observed probability of takeover was identified by Bartley and Boardman in 1986.

The Marris model is also of interest because it focuses on the vulnerability of a firm to agency costs. The valuation ratio V is used to identify the best growth rate that is acceptable to both shareholders and management. U1 to U4 are management indifference curves. They represent the third or Z variable. In the classic Marris model, the third variable is managerial satisfaction or utility. U4 provides the highest utility to management. However, because U4 is beyond the BGP, it is unachievable. Moving to the left of U4 generates a tangency point Y on

Figure 4.2
Marris' Trade-off

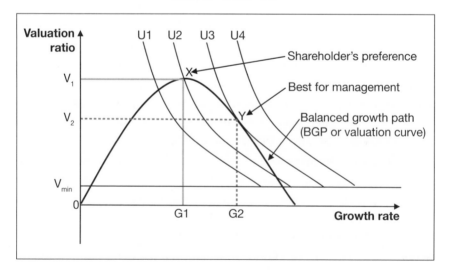

U3, which is tangent to the BGP. It provides the highest possible utility to management. However, point X on U2 provides the best return to shareholders because of a higher valuation ratio. In choosing between these two points, management have a bias to set G2 as their ultimate growth objective. The difference (V_2-V_1) is a measure of agency costs; they can be minimised by PLT.

Quasi-Marris Model of the 21st Century

In his original model, Marris advocated that corporate growth could be manipulated to maintain an optimum dividend-to-profit retention ratio that keeps the shareholders satisfied, yet does not retain too high a level of profit which will create a cash-rich business that is ripe for a takeover. This implies a degree of control over share value that would seem difficult to sustain for even the most effective management team. There are too many factors that could affect the valuation ratio of the business beyond corporate growth. Hence, deciding on how best to achieve growth becomes a crucial issue for management during the life cycle of a firm.

For example, if management wish to grow through product diversification, there is a constraint inherent in the Marris model — the g_d equation — that is fairly acute for firms that opt to do so rather than through acquisition:

$$g_d = f.(d,k)$$
$$\text{growth} = f.(\text{retained profits})$$

where d is the dividend rate as a signal and the parameter k represents the percentage of successful new products. Ultimately, the k parameter depends on R&D, advertising and promotion; the spend on these variables depends on profits, which in turn depends on the efficiency of the firm.

A Marris type would seek to achieve organic growth through product diversification by investing more in R&D and paying less dividends to shareholders. There will be a trade-off between these two variables. Therefore, we have defined the trade-off variables as R&D expenditure and dividends. The third variable, valuation (V), is measured by

$$\text{Marris V} = \frac{\text{Market value}}{\text{Asset value}}$$

$$= \text{Tobin's q}$$

As asset value (net book value) grows with R&D investment in g_d and more shareholders invest in the company on the strength of the PLT, the V increases. Profitability — measured by our earlier equation — should also increase.

The Marris V

The Marris V is an important variable. It is not unrelated to Tobin's q. If $q = V < 1$, the assets are not fully utilised in the company and it would be a good investment to buy shares when $V < 1$. The buying of shares would increase the share price and the market value in time period $t+1$. There are many financial performance ratios, such as the Hamada equations, Sharpe ratio, Jensen alpha, Traynor ratio and Sortino ratio, in addition to alpha and beta of the capital asset pricing model. They represent a measure of financial elasticity by measuring financial performance. The Marris V does likewise, as it measures the elasticity of asset value to market value. However, it is defined in terms of management type to ensure that growth (g_d) determines value (V). The Marris security parameter, a, is a combination of a range of key financial indicators, such as leverage ratio, liquidity ratio and retention ratio. Fundamentally, management are secure if the firm carries minimal debt, delays dividends in time period t in favour of R&D in time period $t+1$ and engages in PLT to reassure investors.

Changes to the availability of information and mismatch in the financial signals make it more difficult to beat the market consistently by observing patterns and actively investing in equities. Data mining and access to large databanks have facilitated the access to real-time data, but the embedded patterns contain nuggets of information which must be decoded. Investors often overlook the patterns or fail to recognise the significance of signals in a game.

The Marris V ratio acts as a buffer when deciding when to buy and sell, and it can be used to enhance returns by market timing as investors plan to exit stocks in order to avoid a bubble. The Marris V is a useful tool for investment based on signals such as dividends or growth, but not market value. The net asset value of Apple Inc is no more linked to its share price than its 700,000 applications. The intellectual capital is more than goodwill which represents the ability of a player in a game to earn an above average return on capital. It should also include a premium on type, playing first mover advantage or second mover advantage and knowing when to reshape strategy in a game. Such intellectual capital might increase the overall valuation of the player; if the player is earning excessive returns on capital, it will invest more capital until Bayesian shareholders are expunged from the shareholder register.

Agency Costs

There is a benchmark rule in Framework T/3: the higher the valuation of a company, the less likely is the threat of a takeover. This rule, however, intimates that dividends should stay high to maintain the share price.

Alternatively, management may wish to invest or trade off more profits to secure more growth with a risk that the value of the company could fall. If the higher valuation was perceived by shareholders to be at a maximum, they would prefer it. Hence, it behoves management to persuade shareholders that the risk of a fall in value can be minimised with a higher growth rate. The inability of management to persuade shareholders gives rise to agency costs because of the separation of ownership and control of a firm.

Berle and Means, who published a classic study in the 1930s, argued that this separation affords management a considerable degree of discretion. The trust between shareholder (as principal) and management (as agent) is threatened if the latter abuse the discretion, and the financial loss to the principal is called an agency cost. One way to tackle agency costs is for management to design a trust mechanism between shareholders and them. This enables shareholders to entrust money to management with a reasonable expectation of getting something back.

Marris Type PLT

A central theme in designing trust is the context of the management decision, that is, how the decision is perceived by shareholders. Shareholders may adopt a Bayesian-type rule, seeing what they want to see about management and the firm. Management should resist this. How? They could signal a PLT to shareholders, where management with prior experience in (games with) value-growth issues introduce positive expectations of a stronger performance (higher value for the firm).

This could be achieved through persuading shareholders to view the decision as a continuum rather than as a dichotomy. That is, it must be framed as a decision about more growth and higher value rather than less value and more growth. Shareholders can then interpret the decision of management as a probability or chance of making a gain by trusting management *versus* that of making a loss.

In terms of the competition, management should evolve as strategic players in that they understand their actions are likely to elicit a reaction from competitors. What this means is that they become conscious of the fact that the price of their product depends on the decisions of their competitors, thereby affecting both the capacity and market reach of the product. For some products, the combination of overcapacity and technology standardisation will drive prices down and create low profit margins. Under these circumstances, management as players engage in patching by re-mapping portions of the product's business to changing market opportunities. The re-mapping is signalled by PLT.

If higher value is sacrificed for higher growth in the interim, one element of the trust mechanism should be that the product becomes **a brand with global reach**, dominating its market through expenditure on R&D and advertising. This combination of decisions is what we define as the diversification acreage. Within the acreage of diversified products, management should spin off a product if it is not achieving its global reach and is underperforming.

Mueller-Marris Hypothesis

Mueller (1972) had advanced the Marris model by advocating a life cycle of firm growth. Mueller's life cycle was a major qualification of the classic linear characterisation of the growth path of a firm advocated by Marris. Borrowing the arguments first identified by Mueller, we can also think of the Marris model as follows. First, sustainable long-term growth requires market growth; this can be achieved by R&D at a cost. In turn, new markets must be supported by new productive capacity. The combined costs of bounded rationality, agency costs, R&D and new capacity may be called the costs of growth. They require cash flow. Cash flow may be obtained from retained profits, new share issues and new debt.

The amount of new debt, in any given period, is constrained on one hand by the unwillingness of lenders to offer unrestricted sums relative to the firm's existing scale and size, and on the other by management's fear of the risks — to them — of excessive leverage. Management can pursue a growth rate (implying specific costs of growth and profit retention ratio) that would maximise the firm's valuation or q-ratio. Alternatively, management may pursue a faster growth rate at the price of reducing the valuation ratio to below its maximum. If management have a growth preference, they should engage in PLT to reassure shareholders that future growth will secure a higher valuation and deliver profits.

It is the trade-off between dividends in time period t and more growth in time period $t+1$ that gives us our first glimpse of this particular Marris type of management who are motivated by achieving sustainable, long-term growth. Management are necessarily risk-averse, as they work out a risk profile (Table 4.1) for all decisions in terms of likely outcomes. Ultimately, the decisions are binary: it is either product X or Y, but not X and Y. The choice of product X carries with it the

Table 4.1
Return/Risk for g_d

	High growth/g_d	Low growth/g_d
Return	Growth drives value Less dividend signals	Value drives growth More dividend signals
Risk	Inability to differentiate fast enough	Innovating at the speed of the slowest firm

opportunity costs — in terms of lost revenues and market shares — of
not selecting product Y. Provided that the costs are minimised, the
contribution of product X to the achievement of sustainable, long-term
growth in the company will be positive.

An understanding of type will help to identify the trade-off facing
a rival competitor. This understanding may enable management to
predict the likely reactions of the competitor, a significant factor in any
competitive, interdependent market structure. In order to understand
management behaviour as observed, we need to know more about
management type. The third variable is key, and there are three possible
candidates:

(1) utility from the classic Marris model,
(2) the valuation ratio from Framework T/3 and
(3) profitability.

The latter was applied to Apple Inc as an exercise in MBA workshops and is illustrated in Figure 4.3, while an estimation of the BGP
of Diageo plc can be found in McNutt (2008).

If the motives of management reveal their type, a Marris type, for
example, may now be summarised as follows: sustainable, long-term
growth requires market growth; this can be achieved by R&D at a cost.

Figure 4.3
Balanced Growth Path for Apple Inc

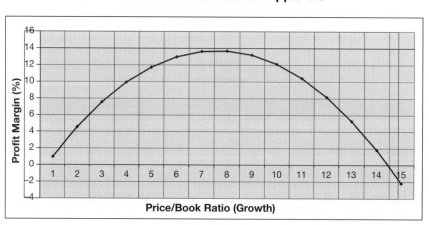

Price/Book Ratio (Growth)

In turn, new markets must be supported by new productive capacity. We advance a quadratic equation to compute the BGP with a $<$ 0:

$$y = a (x - h)^2 + k$$

The BGP in time period $t+1$ can expand or contract and move up or down. The costs of growth in $t+1$ can be explained by the combined costs of the Penrose effect, R&D and new capacity. They require a cash flow or leverage, or both.

A cash flow may be obtained from retained profits, new share issues and new debt. If the company does not borrow externally, the only source of finance to achieve growth is retentions. Herein lies what we shall refer to as a Marris trade-off: **more** R&D requires more cash and may mean **less** to shareholders in the form of dividend payout. Therefore, growth is a function of retained profit.

Marris Signalling

The Z-variable signals a Marris type. Table 4.2 shows three interpretations of Z. Its variations were also tested in Diageo plc and Apple Inc. In the Marris type, we have advocated value V — the market capitalisation of the company divided by its asset (new book) value — as the Z variable. Management of Marris type will signal value maximisation through g_d growth maximisation as the key variable. Signals can be read

Table 4.2
Marris' Third Variable

Variable X	Variable X	Variable Y	Third Variable, Z
Classic Marris	g_d	Dividends	V
Diageo plc case (McNutt, 2008)	g_d	Share price	V
Apple Inc (see Figure 4.3)	Price/Book ratio	Profit margin	Profitability

from listening to interviews with CEOs. As equity traders and analysts become more sophisticated in analysing volatility in the equity markets, management may become less concerned about reaching the third variable level and may be more concerned about signalling their intent to do so. During periods of great movement in equity price, analysts' predictions and management signals will feed off each other so that a signalling maximum could be reached for the share price, p, at

$$\frac{(\sqrt{p})}{p^{-1}}$$

For example, a share of number 9 (£9 or €9) could reach a signalling maximum of 27. The author is examining the significance, if any, of this number. Most analysts are bullish on companies with a price/earnings ratio in the range of 8 to 10 and a dividend yield of 5 per cent. Equity becomes an attractive investment with relatively lower price/earnings ratios. The numbers send a signal. A signalling maximum recognises the fact that a signal is already in the price. For example, companies with expensive shares that then have a profit downgrade — as analysts' targets are not met in time period t — may not necessarily experience a fall in the price of shares as investors await target announcements in time period t+1. A good stock to buy is one that is well-placed to weather the storm of mis-signalling as analysts lag behind CEOs who engage in PLT. In the classic Marris model, there is mention of a security parameter, a, and it may be possible to rewrite it in terms of the capitalised value determined by the signalling share price maximum:

$$a = \frac{\text{Signalling maximum valuation}}{\text{Replacement cost of net assets}}$$

This would allow us to combine the three ratios of Marris V, Tobin's q and profitability, p, as a measure of stock market value. If we were to exclude financial stocks and intangible assets such as brand value or intellectual property rights from the computation of replacement costs, a value of $a = v = q < 1$ might indicate a 'buy'.

The signalling strategy can be interpreted as buying equity at t < T and then selling at t > T, which gives a long position in the dividends paid out in time period T. Higher-yielding stocks with PLT — paying out a higher proportionate dividend — should deliver a much bigger total return in T. Shareholders may prefer a share buyback to the uncertain pay-off from an investment programme. PLT is about reassuring shareholders that no unnecessary risks are being taken and about participating in the market-as-a-game.

An inverse demand for dividends is embedded in Figure 4.3. There is a network effect of more investment from retained profits; the effect dominates the willingness to accept a level of dividends because less dividends equate with more investment which, in turn, equates with more dividends and more investment. If we define the arithmetic mean of the Marris V as $\bar{V}$, we can advance a mean reversion investment guide on equity as follows:

(1) If $V < \bar{V}$, buy.
(2) If $V > \bar{V}$, sell.

The author is considering the possibility of testing an equity valuation equation as follows:

$$N = a0 + a1.\bar{V} + a2.PR + a3\,[V - \bar{V}] + \epsilon$$

where N is the normalised price earnings ratio and PR is the payout ratio or dividends per share/earnings per share.

Any deviation of earnings per share from a trend would alert the intelligent investor to the ability of management to execute strategy in a game. In the game, it is preferable for profits to fall because the player has engaged in an investment programme, and not because management's short-term planning has resulted in the player's product lagging behind in differentiation.

Cost Technology

Feel the force, Luke: let go of your
conscious self and act on instinct.
—**Star Wars**

Competition has changed. Once, there was a reliance on price and quantity, the two classic firm-specific variables. Now, it is quality and innovation, which are quintessentially firm *non-specific* as the firm must provide both because consumers benefit directly from them. A key parameter is the level of consumer demand for the product. In a zero-sum world, for example, one firm could be challenged to meet extra demand due to the falling sales of its rival. Whatever the reason for the extra demand, management strive to set the production rate to match consumer demand. This just-in-time approach can result in waste elimination and lead time reduction. Historically, batch production is considered optimal due to long machine changeover times and the requirement for immediate satisfaction of customer demand. This can involve high stock holding costs for the firm. Production smoothing is the process of adapting the production rate match customer demand. From management's perspective, a high-quality product is still delivered to market on time at greatly reduced costs.

In neoclassical models, the production technology in a company is presented as the constraint imposed on achieving optimal firm size. In Framework T/3, there is no optimal size; rather, the growth of the company depends on the abilities and capabilities of management. If the management are not performing, the company fails in its objectives. Bounded rationality is one reason advanced to explain management underperformance. In this chapter, we advance the idea that management are faced with a capacity constraint which they do not fully understand. The reason for this is a failure to further understand the cost technology embedded in production.

There is a greater need to improve the lines of communication between the production, procurement and sales divisions in a company, be it manufacturing or service-oriented. Otherwise, management will be faced with a production–demand dilemma. One way to overcome this dilemma and obtain a sustainable cost advantage — as a cost leader (CL) — is to understand cost technology. Cost technology is broken down into five constituent steps in this chapter; management can decide which step applies to their company at time period t. The steps can be followed in sequence and may take up to seven years to complete. In the case of Canon, which is illustrated in Figure 5.1, the process took ten years — a period that saw the emergence of Canon as a formidable CL-type player for copiers, scanners, printers and cameras with a sustainable cost advantage in its market.

Figure 5.1
Canon and Cost Leadership Type

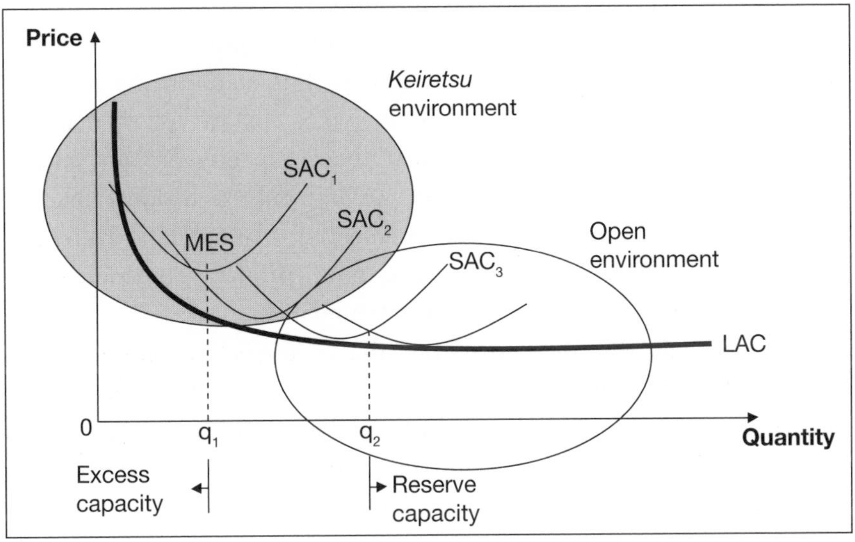

LAC = Long-run average cost, MES = Minimum efficient scale, SAC = Short-run average cost

Production–Demand Dilemma

For management, an understanding of capacity is key to ensuring cost efficiency throughout the production process. Framework T/3 focuses on the link between the cost and product curves. It also distinguishes between excess capacity and reserve capacity. To obtain cost efficiencies, management must be prepared to allow production to determine demand. Why? If demand determines production in a product market with innovation and increasing product differentiation, there is a risk that sales will lag as consumers opt to purchase the latest innovative product. A company with lagging sales will carry inventory and risk carrying obsolete products in a market with ever-changing consumer preferences. Therefore, in the 21st century, many companies risk carrying excess capacity as they are unable to sell what they have produced, simply because consumers no longer prefer their products. This becomes more acute in those markets where innovation, technology and product differentiation are key drivers of demand. One way to escape this dilemma is to engineer the production process such that production determines demand.

Against that background, we introduce the cost leadership model. It has five strategic steps that act as a filter to help identify the cost leadership (CL) type of player. To achieve this status in its industry, management must ensure that a number of steps are followed in the company. We adopt the premise that the companies are not single-plant, single-product manufacturers serving only a national market. This may be the case for a small engineering plant, but globally cost leadership is obtained in multi-plant, multi-product companies that transcend national or regional market boundaries.

Collectively, the five steps define the production relationship in a firm. Step 1 distinguishes between economies of scale and economies of size. Size should be interpreted as a global economy of scale that is achieved when management neutralise the zero-sum constraint. Step 2 focuses on maximising the average productivity of labour, since the measure of average productivity is the inverse of the average variable cost of production. Step 3 requires the introduction of a normalised wage system in the company, offering incentives to the workforce so that a reduction in the number of employees is carefully matched by an increase in productivity.

Step 4 is key. It is about controlling costs: once costs are controlled or fixed during the production cycle, management can focus on decreasing the average fixed cost. This can be achieved by hedging raw materials required during the production cycle, offering workers a fixed term or fixed term-fixed wage contract, outsourcing or rebalancing costs back to suppliers in the supply chain. Finally, step 5 requires management to identify the capacity constraints in the company and to clearly demarcate excess capacity from reserve capacity at each plant in the production technology. Reserve capacity requires the building of additional capacity in the plant in anticipation of demand; excess capacity should be avoided — it can arise if the company is unable to differentiate its products fast enough in an ever-changing consumer market. The ideal outcome is one of zero excess capacity with a reserve capacity in production.

Wage Normalisation

From the geometry of the product and cost curves, we observe an inverse relationship as follows:

$$AVC = \frac{w}{AP_L}$$

In this equation, the average variable cost (AVC) is inversely related to a measure of average productivity (AP_L) depending on the wage level, w. It is a simple observation, but one that can be easily overlooked by management. For example, the management at TooBig plc have decided that 7,000 employees is too big a number to sustain as they search for cost efficiencies. Hence, they decide to downsize to 4,000 employees with a plan to lay off 3,000 employees. This is usually achieved with generous redundancy payments.

In many cases, the most productive employees accept the package on offer. After a while, management at Smaller plc — now with 4,000 employees — realise that they are not achieving their cost reduction objectives. In fact, costs have increased in real terms at Smaller plc. One reason for this is that, on average, the remaining 4,000 employees are not as productive as the 7,000 were. The 7,000 employees included the 3,000 most productive workers who took the redundancy package and ended up being re-employed by Smaller plc on a fixed-fee contract. What this means is that costs are increasing at Smaller plc because productivity has fallen. This is not the only explanation for increasing costs, but it is often a contributor.

It would have been more judicious for TooBig plc to focus on the productivity issue by encouraging the most productive staff through the use of incentives and persuading the least productive workers to leave the plant. It is important to note that average productivity can increase if existing workers are more productive, so that $q^* > q$ for a given number of workers, L. Hence, $q^*/L > q/L$ and productivity has increased because output has increased to q^*. This contrasts with the more conventional approach which reduces the number of workers from L to L^* in the belief that $q/L^* > q/L$. Sadly, this result may not occur. Productivity falls as the level of output, q, does not increase; q will also not increase if the most productive workers leave. Management should remember that the total product of L produced on a fixed amount of K is the same as the average product of K when L is fixed. If we assume that when K is fixed its value is 1, and when L is fixed its value is also 1, the following relationship holds:

$$AP_L = TP_K, \text{ when } K = 1$$

With a normalised wage structure, there is a greater focus on productivity as it offers incentives to the most productive workers to stay and the least productive staff to leave. There could be share options, for example, and a range of productivity incentive contracts present in the plant. A normalised wage sets $w = 1$, and we have

$$AVC = \frac{1}{AP_L}$$

Therefore, notwithstanding how costs are reduced, sustainable cost advantage can be obtained only if there is an increase in productivity as a consequence of the cost-reduction measures.

Excess Capacity *versus* Reserve Capacity

During the production phase, it is important for management to understand the capacity constraints facing a modern production facility. We distinguish between excess capacity and reserve capacity. For each plant size, there is a minimum efficient scale of operation (MES). At this point, average costs are at a minimum; production beyond this point will give rise to diseconomies of scale and rising costs. However, production is often at a level to the left of the MES plant size. Traditionally, this is the point of excess capacity; the older arguments developed in economics had accused the monopolist of producing with excess capacity. Why bother to produce more (towards the MES output) when there was no other rival supplier in a monopolist's market?

However, modern firms today — and not in a monopoly position — can be producing with excess capacity because they are faced with an ever-increasing demand for their product at a time when they are unable to product-differentiate fast enough to meet that demand. Technically, they have spare capacity in the plant, which translates into excess capacity with a slack demand for the firm's product. Unless the firm is able to differentiate its product in the market, it will be producing at a point to the left of its MES with excess capacity. This is equivalent to *capacite excedentaire*. This is not a preferred position — for management to be located to the left of the MES — because it is simply not cost-efficient.

Conversely, reserve capacity arises during production when the long-run marginal cost is zero. It is best to think of reserve capacity as **installed capacity** that is used by management when it is required. This means that different levels of production can be reached at zero marginal cost. This is because the company has built in additional capacity into the production process early on in the production cycle. Such a situation could arise in a product market where **production determines demand**: this is very relevant for the management of innovative products such as mobile phones, printers and video game consoles.

Reserve capacity — shown by the dark-coloured L-shape line in Figure 5.2 — defines the long-run average cost (LAC). In economics, we refer to it as the level of production where constant returns to scale prevail for the LAC, as illustrated in Figure 5.2. However, it is more interesting when the L-shape line neither increases upward (looking like an elongated U-shape) nor trends downward (representing a declining LAC), as illustrated in Figure 5.3. In this case, the cost structure implies that output is not large enough to observe whether average costs will rise. Management may prefer to be cautious and not push production too far in case costs increase.

Figure 5.2
Shape of Cost Curves

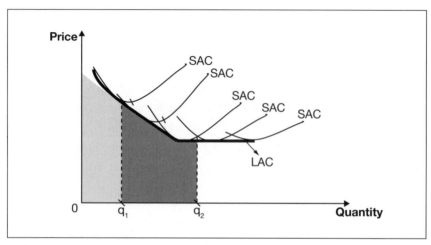

LAC = Long-run average cost, SAC = Short-run average cost

Figure 5.3
Declining Long-run Average Cost

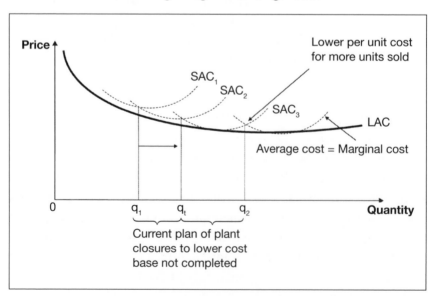

LAC = Long-run average cost, SAC = Short-run average cost

Cost Leader Type

The demand (for a product) may be so demanding — what we call **reserve capacity on demand** or CoD — that it is better for the manufacturer to allow production to control demand. This contracdicts the conventional wisdom that it is demand that drives production. Arguably, it may be more cost-efficient to engineer a plant with reserve capacity so that production determines demand.

Functionalities are precisely what consumers are demanding. For example, a printer is a printer + copier + scanner + fax machine. Or a mobile phone is a telephone + MP3 player + mega-pixel camera + email communications device. The combination of different functionalities $(q_1, q_2, \ldots q_n)$ generates **economies of scope** at step 1, such that

$$C(q_1, q_2) < C(q_1) + C(q_2)$$

It is more cost-efficient for management to have one large plant that produces a printer, a copier and a printer + copier than to have three separate plants.

Once a plant has reached its size, economies of scope can be incorporated into the cost technology. However, this may take time. If so, the time component should be signalled to the market. If there are any production delays, they should be signalled as shipment delays and not a failure to meet demand. The signal is necessary in order to calm investors while allowing management to plan for additional capacity at the production plant(s). Consequently, management are in a stronger position to control costs. What one observes is a flat-bottomed cost curve; with seasonality in demand or a new innovative product on demand, the company with reserve capacity in production will be better placed to meet that demand at cost-efficient levels of production. When observed implementing the five steps outlined in the checklist on the following page, the firm is more likely to emerge as a CL type in the game.

A key assumption in Figure 5.3 is that a player can change plant size. This can occur due to economies of scale when the firm upgrades from a small plant to a larger plant. The minimum point on the LAC

Checklist: Five-Step Analysis

STEP 1: Distinguish between Economies of **Scale**, Economies of **Size** and Economies of **Scope** in the production process:

- *Scale*: $\Delta K = \Delta L = 2\%$ and $\Delta q > 2\%$

- *Size:* Achievable in competitive market $\Delta q = 4\%$ in phase 1; decide ex-post in phase 2 of the production process the most optimal, ΔK or ΔL; and implement in phase 3.

- *Scope:* Across production so that $C(q_1, q_2) < C(q_1) + C(q_2)$.

STEP 2: Focus on increasing average productivity of labour, AP_L. How? Note that

$$AP_L = \frac{w}{AVC}$$

where w is the wage proxy and AVC are the average variable costs.

STEP 3: Normalise the wage structure; let $w = 1$. Offer workers incentives or bonus payments as productivity increases, revisit the organisational structure and consider the production process as a nexus of contracts.

STEP 4: Control more of the production costs, that is, allow all the costs to be controlled. Hedge positions on material inputs, minimise exchange rate risks and have workers on fixed-wage, fixed-term contracts with incentives (such as flexible manufacturing).

STEP 5: Demarcate excess capacity (idle capacity) from reserve capacity (installed capacity), bearing in mind that excess capacity can occur if the product is not sufficiently differentiated fast enough in the market to capture market sales. At the point of production in phase 1, ensure sufficient installed capacity to meet demand in later phases of production.

is the **optimum scale of plant**, the MES. SAC represents the cost structure of the smaller plant; the corresponding minimum point on the SAC is the **optimum rate of output**. The challenge for management is to move from optimum rate of output to optimum scale of plant. Division and specialisation of labour can bring about economies of scale; likewise, the adoption of advanced technology — such as robotics and computer technology — can trigger off economies of scale.

Today, management seek to obtain economies of scale in the supply chain by outsourcing to a lower-wage economy, such as the move from the European Union to the economies of Brazil, Russia, India and China in equipment manufacture, textiles and back-office financial administration. However, management must ensure that productivity does not decrease at the outsourced plants: simply offering lower wages does reduce variable costs, but average costs will decline only if productivity is increased. As output increases, management are faced with a second challenge of understanding the capacity constraints that may emerge during the production process.

Arguably, management intent on cost leadership will not produce at the minimum point on an SAC curve. If they did, they would lose in the sense that they could still produce at a lower average cost with a slightly larger but underutilised plant if it were to the left of the minimum point of the LAC, and with a slightly smaller but over-utilised plant if it were to the right of the low point of the LAC curve. This is McNutt's dilemma: Do management build a larger plant that may be underutilised, or retain the existing plant that may be over-utilised? The dilemma cannot be solved unless management introduce a normalised wage structure and demarcate the point at which present production levels are in terms of capacity. The economic argument is simply that the cost curve derives its shape because of the five CL-type steps.

Ex Nihilo Nihil Fit

Rational management know the old adage that 'nothing comes from nothing'; hence, a decision must be taken. For example, Brand Inc in time period t could signal the launch of a new product in time period t+1 and allow a 'word of mouth' moon-shot to exist in the market.

Thus, consumers who want to purchase the product in time period t find that it is not available. Demand is not determining the production. It is by signalling that Brand Inc is able to create a **ghost demand** in time period t that the production cycle in t+1 can be engineered to meet that level of demand. However, it is the production at time period t+1 that ultimately determines demand at t+1.

This back-scatter approach to production is characteristic of a CL type at step 5. The risk in delaying production is the loss of a first mover advantage (FMA) in a product with a growing demand for its functionalities. However, the gain in observing another player succumbing to demand — as a product underperforms due to lagging consumer expectations — is the second mover advantage (SMA). In the production game, there are two conjoint decisions:

(1) FMA loss < SMA gain
(2) FMA gain > SMA loss

CL type is not about an obsession with cost cutting *per se*, that is, ensuring that every purchase — no matter how small — is logged into a central accounting system. CL type is about mistake-proofing against these two decisions. Mistake-proofing can be assisted by a regret matrix (Chapter 10) which computes the opportunity cost or loss of deviating from an optimal decision.

Increases in efficiency should be looked at in terms of a marginal decrease in costs due to engineering or technology solutions. The reserve capacity depicted in Figure 5.1 refers to capacity that is in excess of the maximum peak demand. For a CL-type player, production-led demand sets the peak demand and the reserve capacity supports the CL player's strategic choice set in the game:

(1) action: absorbs the output of a rival firm who exits the game;
(2) action: engages in predatory tactics by increasing output, thus proliferating products in the market with the express intent of forcing a rival player to exit; or
(3) no action: signals capacity as a *credible threat* in a limit pricing game, thus delaying the entry of a new player. We discuss this option in the following chapter.

Limit Pricing and Vertical Blending

You tremble, carcass, but you would tremble still more if you knew where I am going to take you.
—Marechal de Turenne

Blending is the coexistence of two types, one observed by signals (management type) and the other displayed in effective action (player type). Vertical blending is an exercise of type rather than a case of structural determination. This assumes that it is in the management's power to act differently (Lukes, 1974). For example, the appointment of a new CEO will introduce a new type of management. Hence, we need to further understand how management type can affect a firm in a manner that complements its interests.

Vertical blending occurs when the type of management influences the type of player. Management type is then embedded in the firm and signalled to the market as a player type. This is important because it links the performance of the company to the type of management. Management are appointed by shareholders or private equity because of their type. Some are known as ruthless cost cutters, some believe in growth by acquisition and others believe in organic growth. The appointment of a new CEO sends a signal to the market; it is for the market — competitors and equity analysts — to identify the management type in order to avoid misreading the signals and actions of the company as a player.

Weak vertical blending occurs when the culture of the firm or company — comprising its stakeholders — influences the type of management by getting the latter to do what they do not want to do through shaping or determining their actions. Activist shareholders prefer to coerce or persuade management to change strategy, such as the recent attempt by the hedge fund company, Greenlight Capital, to seek greater returns for Apple Inc's shareholders. As a player, rational management may simply duplicate the reasoning process of the stakeholders. However, taking control is an irreducible fact because it emanates from the control of information within the organisation *per se* and through the game process. As the game unfolds, management's actions ultimately define the type of player the company has become in the game.

Signalling

When management realise that they have the power to act differently — and they do act differently — blending is complete. Therefore, the process arises when management's actions mean something to them as individuals. That is, they are capable of processing their own experience in a manner that confound all predictions by a near rival — predictions that are based on the fact finder's observations or the near rival's description of type of management. The difficulty for management lies in trying to understand the blend in a rival firm. It is difficult to cope with the blend as it may be due to the fact that the type of management *per se* was formed — during the game — in reaction to competitors.

The key issue is to provide a template on how management can best represent the blend created in the company in actions or words. To do so is to understand the words and actions of management: the signals. The template is based on player interdependence in a game. While the actions are interdependent — such as in a sequential pricing game of leader-follower — the signals by which they are prompted are mutually independent. This is because player actions mean something to management as individuals; different management will interpret the same signal differently. Consequently, we refer to taking an action as the observed reality: the game success or pay-off — the Porterian competitive advantage — is obtained from knowing when and how to act.

Game Situation

The type of player arises from an economic foundation based on a theory of oligopoly. Oligopoly is a market structure characterised by a few players, usually fewer than five. The number is significant: with so few players, there is greater interdependency amongst the players and a greater probability that one of them will recognise this and try to exploit it. The object is to maximise the economic position of the player — the pay-off — and to obtain a preferred outcome for all players, that is, the market.

In oligopoly markets, we are more likely to observe a consolidation across the market shares of the players in time period t+1. We make this assumption for the purposes of this book. Consolidation is the point at which the zero-sum constraint becomes acute.

A fact finder will observe constant market shares. Player A's loss of market share from 35.2 per cent to 35 per cent translates into a gain for player B. For game theory to become an analysis tool, the underlying environment must not change too fast so that we can equate management behaviour in terms of an equilibrating behaviour. It means player A realises that the range 35 per cent to 35.2 per cent is the best market share obtainable given the likely reaction to their action from other players in the market-as-a-game. Hence, player A does nothing to regain the 0.2 per cent market share that was lost because there is a probability of losing 0.2 per cent. When player A realises this outcome, we are at a Nash equilibrium. The realisation may be due to the fact that one of the players may have played a game in an earlier time period.

When decision making is interdependent, the outcome accruing to one player from an action will be co-dependent on the reaction of another player. When players take cognisance of their mutual inter-dependence, a time will come in the game when there is no unilateral incentive to deviate from an agreed position. Therefore, when companies take cognisance of their mutual interdependence, they become players in the market-as-a-game and the game dimension is described by geography, space and product-process technology.

Players are ascribed a type by opponents based on observed patterns of behaviour — the signals that represent a sequence of moves in the game. Game theory is about rational people interacting with each other in a way that helps them to achieve their own goals. This branch of game theory is non-cooperative game theory; while the rules of the game are pre-determined, players can consider the consequences of different types of rules as the **game situation** creates a mechanism on how the game can be played. Gurven (2004) noted that people can become more or less likely to cooperate depending on the type of cooperation required. For example, a group may readily cooperate in fishing, but not in conservation. Business may cooperate in innovation, but not in price fixing or market share allocation. Therefore, the context in which the game is played — the game situation — plays an important role in players' preferences and behaviour.

One-Shot Move

Player A decides to reduce price. The key is whether player B will react to any price movement. If A believes that B will react, it is imperative for A to have a reply to the likely reaction from B. Hence, we have the strategy triangle of action-reaction-reply. If A does not have a Nash reply, it is because A did not expect a reaction.

The key to understanding our definition of strategy in Framework T/3 is to ask: Why did A not expect a reaction? What is it about B's pattern of behaviour that led A to believe that B would not react to any price change from A? One factor is B's type, defined in terms of the type of player and type of management.

Type of management refers to the subjective behaviour of management in terms of a preference for pricing or organic growth. Type of player is to be understood in terms of the patterns of observed behaviour of the company in the market. For example, we seldom observe price wars between Pepsi and Coca-Cola in their core market, unlike Sony, Nintendo and Sega who experienced a lengthy price war in the video games market in the 1990s.

A key question is: Given their strategy, how should they behave? For example, player A reduces price to correct declining total revenue, but competitor B does not know the reason why the observed price has fallen. Could player A be a Baumol type? If so, the price move observed is a **one-shot move** and may not require a reaction from player B. To avoid any misunderstanding, player A could signal its type as a Baumol type. Type and belief about a competitor's next move are integral parts of a limit pricing entry analysis.

Limit Pricing Model

Also known as the Bain-Modigliani model, the limit pricing model defines a game between an incumbent type and a camouflaged entrant type. To understand player type, we use the Bain-Modigliani or limit pricing model.

The limit pricing model (see Figure 6.1) represents the classic example where a player considering entry into a new market is

Figure 6.1
The Bain-Modigliani (Limit Pricing) Model

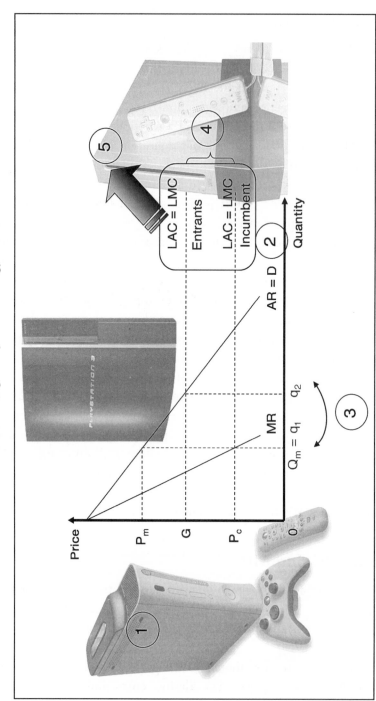

AR = Average revenue, D = Demand, G = Entrant's breakeven price (limit price), LAC = Long-run average cost, LMC = Long-run marginal cost, MR = Marginal revenue, P_c = Perfectly competitive price, P_m = Monopoly price, Q_m = Monopoly output

presented as a demonstration of non-cooperative game theory. The biggest uncertainty faced by the new entrant is predicting the reaction of the incumbent player in the market, whose perceived options are to either be accommodating and allow entry or to react aggressively with price cuts to G or P_c in Figure 6.1. Later in Chapter 9, in Figure 9.4 we analyse the price war between the incumbent (Sony) and an entrant (Microsoft) in the video games and consoles market.

In a limit pricing model, a rational incumbent is more likely to cede market share to avoid a price war. If the decision is taken not to enter the market, the pay-off for the new entrant will be zero and the incumbent retains full value of the game (10) in Figure 6.2. Should the company decide to enter, the incumbent has two strategies to pursue: retaliate with aggressive price cuts, thereby risking a price war that will leave it with a reduced pay-off of 2, or accommodate.

In Figure 6.2, the new entrant cannot afford such a price war and will fail to return a profit from the venture (losing 7). If the incumbent accommodates the new entrant, its pay-off is reduced to 8 through ceding market share to the newcomer who makes a successful entry with a profit of 5. Self-interest (profit maximisation) governs the likely response of the market incumbent, thereby negating the value of any probability calculation if the incumbent's first response is to prevent entry. While it is sufficient to analyse the probability of the reaction options, it is necessary to be guided by what actions the rational, self-interested respondent is likely to reply with in the game.

Retaliation

The reply will depend on the player's belief about the type of player the competitor is in a game. Like the Galton's ox weight contest, each player will observe how individual errors and biases in predicting likely reactions will tend to cancel each other out as the sought-after information about type is distilled in some aggregate measure of belief. Players will choose whether to adopt a binary approach:

Player A asks:
(1) Binary: Will player B react? Yes or No
(2) Non-binary: Player B will react; probability = X%

Figure 6.2
Market Entry Decision — Extensive Form

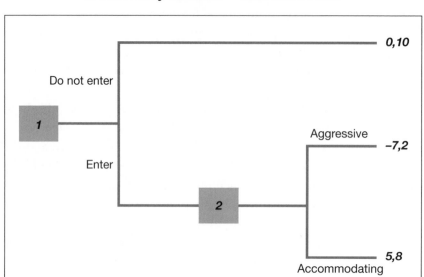

Notice that in Figure 6.2, each option open to the rival results in a change in the total value of the game. Retaliation would lead to a price war in which lower profits would devalue the total returns available to all players. In this example, the resulting market losses are 5. Alternatively, allowing the new company to enter would grow the overall market value to 13 — the sum of the pay-offs 5 and 8. The strategies open to the players are clear. Notice that the first decision lies with the new entrant; the subsequent response by the incumbent makes this a sequential game. Outlining the strategies forms the key to systematic thinking about which strategy is the optimal path to follow.

Limit Pricing Strategy Set

Do not enter, do not retaliate (status quo)
Enter and retaliate
Enter and accommodate

Dominant Strategy: Player 2 (Incumbent Type)

The same game can be represented in a pay-off matrix form. This is illustrated in Figure 6.3. The game matrix directs the players to a strategic choice. Player 1 assumes that player 2 will act in rational self-interest; it is in player 2's interest to assume the reciprocal arrangement applies. Suppose there is a first strategy that 'under no circumstances yields a lower pay-off and sometimes does better' than a second option. We said that the first strategy **dominates** the second. In Figure 6.2, player 1 may have a dominant strategy. If they do not enter, they will have no pay-offs. The incumbent does not need to react and will retain the market value. The 'do not enter' strategy only dominates the 'enter' strategy if the incumbent threatens to engage in a price war. A zero pay-off is better than a loss of 7, but can the entrant trust the incumbent?

However, for player 1, the 'accommodating' strategy of the incumbent would result in a higher pay-off for the new entrant than not entering at all. With mistrust, player 1 has no dominant strategy.

Figure 6.3
Market Entry Pay-offs: — Normal Form

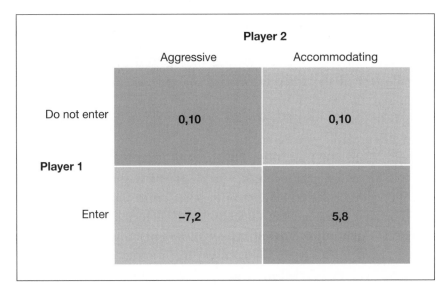

	Player 2	
	Aggressive	Accommodating
Do not enter	0,10	0,10
Player 1		
Enter	–7,2	5,8

Player 2, however, has a dominant strategy. In both cases of 'do not enter' and 'enter', the incumbent is better off accommodating the new entrant. This is indicated by the pay-off of 10 if the newcomer does not enter, and a higher pay-off of 8 *versus* a pay-off of 2 if player 2 accommodates. In this scenario, accommodation strategy dominates the aggressive retaliation strategy. The optimum strategy in this game is that player 1 — knowing the pay-offs (as opposed to the probabilities) — realises it is in player 2's best interest to accommodate and will therefore enter the market.

Player Types and Signals

Markets characterised by incumbent management who regard a threat of entry as an actual plan of entry at a time period yet to be decided can be described as contestable. A contestable market is as close as we get to the textbook competition. However, as geography begins to define market boundaries, incumbents face the possibility of a *de novo* entrant type. A *de novo* **type** is a player in the same geographic market as the incumbent in at least two product markets that complement a third product market, the incumbent's market. The *de novo* type seeks to gain synergy and acquires the incumbent. Hence, a *de novo* entrant type grows through acquisition as the boundaries of the market expand. The boundaries can expand due to technology, innovation or change in regulations. With changes in technology at time period t, a player can exit a game and return in time period t+1. Netscape, for example, exited the Internet browser war against Microsoft but has re-entered the market-as-a-game as Mozilla and is competing with incumbent players Google and Apple's Safari. This is a good example of a **newborn** player who re-enters the game as technology changes. For example, from 2002 to 2006, Kodak could be defined as a newborn when it adopted digital technology in its products after witnessing the digital revolution that had swept through the camera market.

For an incumbent, the difficulty lies in determining whether the entrant is a **potential entrant type** with no intention to enter in time period t or a *de novo* type who has every intention to enter. Depending on the management's belief, actions will differ on how best to limit entry. Each action will act as a signal to other players in the market and may invite a reaction from other incumbent players. For example, if an incumbent type believes with a high probability that entry will happen, it reduces its pre-entry price. This triggers off a reaction from the incumbent players who have lost a price differentiation advantage.

Believable Bills

The incumbent type is easily recognised as an endogenous, historic player already in the market because of, say, government imprimatur, national geography or survival in the market-as-a-game. A defining characteristic of an incumbent type is protection of market share. This requires effort and management time to delay or prevent entry by an entrant type. Vertical blending with such players creates 'believable Bills' (bB) based on the belief that if entrants enter the market, profits post-entry would be driven to zero. The bB will do everything to delay, retard or prevent entry. Accommodation is not a dominant strategy for the bB type (see Table 6.1).

Entrant types, by definition, seek entry. They are sub-divided into potential entrant types who threaten to enter at a point in time and *de novo* entrant types who do enter at a point in time. The difficulty for an incumbent type at a point in time lies in determining the type of entrant. The incumbent management's belief of the entrant's type of management will determine its pre-entry actions.

Table 6.1
Player Types

	Incumbent action Believable Bill	Probability of entry Doubting Thomas
Potential entrant type	Reduce price Increase output	High and incorrect Low and correct
***De Novo* entrant type**	Dividends policy Increase share price	High and incorrect Low and correct

Doubting Thomas

The entrant type will signal to the incumbent type its intention to enter the latter's market. This gives rise to the 'doubting Thomas' (dT) incumbent who does not perceive the threat of entry at a point in time. The dT knows how the entrant will act because he knows the entrant management will act rationally. However, the entrant is a player; if its signals are deviant, dT may not be able to respond when the entrant actually enters the market. If the bB incumbent believes that the entrant type will actually enter the market, the incumbent management will take actions to deter entry. For example, they may reduce the market price or increase the quantity produced in the pre-entry period.

However, if the potential entrant type has no intention to enter in time period t, the bB incumbent has reacted to a threat of entry that will not materialise at time period t. If an incumbent management behave in such a manner, they would have believed that the threat of entry was credible. This means that there was a high probability that the entrant type would have entered, which explained the rationale for reducing the market price. Conversely, a dT incumbent would not have reduced the price upon a threat of entry, but at the higher price it may have exposed itself to price differentiation by other players. They include incumbent players who may opt to exploit the price differences.

Rank and Type

If all incumbents share the same belief, the low price will signal to the entrant that the incumbent expects entry in time period t and believes that the entrant is a *de novo* type. This means there is a probability of entry at time period t. Earlier, we distinguished between bB and dT: bB's reaction is to prevent entry whereas dT dismisses the threat at this point in time. Conversely, if the incumbent player initiates a signalling game with an aggressive dividends policy, this may be interpreted as a signal of the presence of a *de novo* entrant in the expanding geographic market. In other words, a bB player who is concerned about a possible threat of takeover may opt to return capital to its shareholders in the form of generous dividends. This would occur if bB management were of the Marris type.

However, if a second incumbent feels threatened by the price action of the first incumbent, there is every possibility that both players could end up in a price war. The players that survive a price war are referred to as **extant** types. A price war may have been the original intention of the entrant type who had earlier signalled its intention to enter the incumbent's market. However, the price war arises simply because one incumbent reduces price in the belief that the entrant is a potential entrant type and is likely to enter at time period $t+1$. Nonetheless, no entry occurs.

Conversely, in the case of a *de novo* entry, for example, one incumbent may place a takeover bid for a second incumbent player, either as a defensive strategy (two incumbents are less likely to be acquired) or by breaking rank. The assumption with rank is that incumbents in a game remain silent until an external shock jolts their market. The shock may manifest itself in the form of new technology, adoption of new innovation or emergence of a *de novo* entrant in an expanding geographic market. A player may have anticipated the external shock and readjusted its decision making to reveal its type as an endogenous, rank-breaking player in the post-shock environment.

An incumbent type, for example, can readjust its actions from any agreed rank; an incumbent that breaks rank is referred to as an **endogenous rival** type. The assumption is that the players in a rank game are able to act jointly because each player observes the behaviour of the others and obeys the rules. Consider a taxi rank, where the rule stipulates that the taxi at the head of the queue goes first and a random customer arriving at the rank is required to join the queue for a taxi. The rank is a good example of rational cooperation that is both desirable from the customer's point of view and sustainable from the player's point of view. A rank may be more acceptable than a cartel because altruistic motives are ascribed to the players. Thus, the players can act jointly in the knowledge that their behaviour will not be condemned by a third party.

In order to understand the behaviour of an endogenous rival type, we need to consider the significance of ascribing altruistic motives to the players. For example, at one time it was regarded to be in the public's interest to have a national monopoly with responsibility for, say, public utilities — a view that has progressed into a national champion theory. Traditionally, national banks have served a national population. With the rise and emergence of a single European market, they begin to rethink their strategy. They can choose to become the target of *de novo* entrants as they expand beyond national geographic boundaries, or they can break rank by acquiring smaller incumbents or adopting new technology faster than other incumbents. This signals an aggressive, organic growth strategy that remained silent under the rules of the rank. However, because we use banks as a fictitious example — and bank behaviour is not immune from antitrust investigation — as players in a game banks would be advised to deny a rank ever existed, notwithstanding the observations of the fact finder (McNutt, 2005).

Why Enter? Predatory Tactics

It may be helpful for management to derive an entry function in order to refocus the debate on the restrictions to entry as follows:

$$E(q) = q^{2m}$$

where $q = [Q - q^*]$, Q is total demand and q^* is incumbent output, or q_1 in Figure 6.1. Of particular interest is the exponent term '2m', which generates the concavity of the entry function. The specification of the entry function and its concavity highlight the restrictive nature of entry. $E(q)$ translates into actual market share if entry was impeded. As the incumbents increase q^*, q tends to 0 and $E(0) = 0$. The function $E = E(q)$ maps the optimal level of exclusion output for each number of entrants. Technology and economies of scale in production make exclusion output easier to produce; this could be interpreted as a fall in the price of exclusion resources. This would also imply a higher return on each dollar spent on exclusion and an upward shift in the function. The equilibrium outcome is one of fewer number of smaller firms than before entry deterrence.

An unanticipated change in technology may have left incumbent players with considerable excess capacity even though demand has not expanded. Alternatively, as argued in Chapter 5, a decline in demand may have left firms with excess capacity. Whatever the reason for excess capacity, suppose the dominant player is matched by an entrant who has the capacity to produce X per cent of output without a significant increase in marginal cost. In this case, the reserve capacity of the entrant would limit the incumbent's efforts to raise price above the marginal cost. Competition policy might argue that the incumbent's excess capacity may make any threat by it to engage in predatory pricing — to keep out new entrants — more credible. If the incumbent monopolist has used real resources to deter entry, the issue that needs to be addressed is how the opportunity cost of those resources factors into the traditional costs of playing a game. New entrants probably would not find an industry operating at excess capacity an attractive one to enter even in the absence of predatory threats. The E(q) function would support this type of outcome, an outcome that requires a debate on credible mechanisms and the Bertrand dilemma that are discussed in Chapter 9.

If a player signals a price reduction post-entry — and has a reputation for reducing price — the lower price signal becomes a *credible threat* only if rival players (entrants, in particular) believe that a lower price is likely post-entry and do not enter. The reputation *per se* of a player informs the belief system of other players in the game. An entrant player with reserve capacity — a CL-type player — could, however, bluff the player who signalled a price reduction by entering the market at the lower signalled price and engage in a price war.

With imperfect signals on type, players observe the 'noise' made by their opponents' actions. If each player observes a noisy signal of the true type, they could end up in a compete *versus* compete outcome — a price war. Hence, an entrant player has to change its prior belief rather than update it, thereby violating Bayes rule because of zero or minimal probability that action (lowering price post-entry) equates with type alone.

If the player is given new information — surprise — that it did not expect, it revises its prior belief. In the limit price signalling model depicted in Figure 6.1, player type is important because it can be observed as an easy-to-process signal defined by the equation

$$\text{Type} = f.(\text{signal})$$

However, if the player's true intention is hidden or camouflaged — or if the credible threat of action hangs over the game like the sword of Damocles — the equation

$$\text{Signal} = f.(\text{type, belief})$$

becomes more relevant in the play. Signals contain a message about type (honesty), and type contains a message about signals (noise). Beliefs now depend on the game play and the context in which the game is played. In other words, players rely more on honesty and trust.

Dark Strategy

*Your words are like the handiwork of my
ancestor Daedalus; and if I were the sayer or
propounder of them, you might say that this
comes of my being his relation and that this is
the reason why my arguments walk away and
won't remain fixed where they are placed.*
—**Socrates**

Competitors know of each other's existence. The zero-sum constraint is acute. In this context, type is not only about conduct and behaviour; it is also about making decisions, carrying them through and taking action. We may regard the courses of action open to management as strategies of the firm. A strategy is one firm's plan of action adopted in the light of management beliefs about the reactions of its competitors. In this scenario, for example, a firm's pricing policy *per se* may not affect the shareholder value; it will, however, affect the value through the management's reaction to the action of a competitor on the original pricing policy.

In other words, management must understand that action leads to a reaction which elicits a reply. Every action must have a (Nash) reply. This hypothesis is maintained throughout the book. It means that management should not be surprised by events in time period $t+1$ that emanate from their action in time period t. As with our opening example in Chapter 1 on the possible launch of a gPhone ahead of the iPhone launch, the signal on the possibility of a gPhone in the market-as-a-game is called a **moon-shot**. A moon-shot is a signal that players deny. However, if one player believes the moon-shot to be credible, they are observed to act sooner than the cost technology or capacity may have facilitated at time period t. It is worth pointing out that the gPhone was launched in September 2008; was the iPhone released too soon in the summer of 2007?

Answers to this type of question fall into the unknown of strategic behaviour — what we refer to as **dark strategy**. Will Nokia enter the laptop market? Will Google enter the smartphone market? These were challenging questions as at September 2009, and their answers could partly be accommodated in Framework T/3. By observing type and understanding the convergence of technologies, players would be in a better position to consider the market that they should be in at time period $t+1$. So, should Apple Inc be in telecoms? Yes!

Mistake-proofing

Launching 'too soon' can be a risk, especially if the player has a capacity constraint in its vertical supply chain. A greater risk — in the absence of a Nash reply — is that competitors can secure a **second mover advantage** (SMA) by emulating the original players' functionalities. Nokia, for example, was in a strong position to secure this advantage in the evolving smartphone market in 2009. By differentiating the music content on its xPress models and focusing on professional users of the N-series and E-series phones, Nokia could have secured a competitive SMA. However, with the arrival of Apple Inc's iPhone 3GS, the emerging Android platform and the suite of HTC smartphones, Nokia's SMA faded away.

Player strategy arises when management realise that they are in a game. In economics, rational man makes optimal choices guided by well-defined and stable preferences. There are preferences on costs — marginal cost pricing, ABC costing and incremental costs. Management are faced with a supply correspondence dilemma: on the one hand, competitors squared off against cyclical consumer preferences; on the other hand, the Penrose effect squared off against internal X-inefficiencies and costs squared off against price positioning. There will be capacity constraints — traditionally referred to as short-run problem — coupled with planning horizon issues in the long run. A decision must translate into action. This is not easy. For example, planned obsolescence, productivity and niche batch production characterise the production technology of many firms. Endogenous rivals whose type is unknown at a given time period may emerge. Thus, the Nash premise becomes more acute. This is the essence of modern competition.

Belief System CV ≠ 0

For management, there are tensions between economic routine and argument and the desire to follow one's own instinct in business. While the company may have a smaller asset base, it is generating greater pre-tax profits. Hence, it is making more profit from the same level of assets as its near-rival. This will be reflected in the stock market as the company has been observed to outperform its near-rival. It is important for management to learn that the best player — in terms of profitability and performance measures — is not necessarily the biggest player in the market. The biggest player is also not necessarily the best. The belief system is captured by conjectural variation (CV) in the following way. If player A has a CV = 0, they do not expect a reaction from a competitor; conversely, with a non-zero CV, a player expects a reaction to their action in a game.

It is this feature that distinguishes knowing a decision has to be made from knowing when and how to make it. Knowing that a decision has to be made is referred to as making a decision; knowing when and how a decision has to be made is referred to as taking an action. The latter term is analogous to making a move in game theory, that is, players make their moves when they decide on the strategy to be adopted. In brief, a strategy is a string of moves or actions.

Therefore, management's subjectivity is an essential property. It refers to their sense of past, present and future which makes them at once a creature of history. Earlier in Chapter 1, we noted that March and Simon (1958) and the behavioural approach have argued that management are bounded rational in decision making, while Penrose (1959) has argued that management are limited in their abilities. Both subscribe to a view that management are exposed to complex information daily and are reliant on subordinates to inform them of the precise usefulness of the information. Nonetheless, management must take the first step in decision making. In doing so, management are guided not only by their instinct, but also by the advice from within the management team and the likely reactions from competitors. This is reminiscent of Poincare's 'collision of ideas' in that it yields something new in a company and a degree of unpredictability for observers of patterns of behaviour. Simple ideas and actions generate more complex ones through a process of vertical blending, whereby the type of management blends with the type of player.

Behaving Strategically

In Chapter 1, we have defined the economics of strategy as a combination of the Penrose effect (PE) and the Nash premise (NP). The latter requires a player to have a reply function as it anticipates a reaction to its action. In their pursuit of growth, for example, management realise that a growth rate implies specific costs and trade-offs. In Mueller's (1972) life cycle interpretation of firm growth, desired growth is often limited by both internal and external constraints. Internally, there are Penrose limitations on the ability of management to achieve growth. This is coupled with external constraints in a zero-sum market where the growth of the firm slows down. Management do not wish for this to happen.

As costs are committed to maximising growth, management insecurity about the impact of the zero-sum constraint could force them to dilute the market value of the company sufficiently to create a reverse risk of takeover. Hence, an understanding of the management type of the competitor becomes crucial. When management take cognisance of a competitor's interdependence, they become a player in a game and decisions are said to be strategic. Management behave strategically when they realise that every decision is followed by an action that is observed by market participants. This gives us a definition of the strategy (S) equation:

$$S = PE + NP$$

It is a combination of minimising the PE and ensuring a response to any reaction to one's initial decision in a game. The PE can be minimised by understanding type, and with a non-zero CV the player has anticipated a reaction. Ideally, as third-party observers — the fact finders — we would like to understand how the decision was achieved and — for each alternative in the decision-making process — to understand why it was rejected, and by whom. In other words, we need to understand the context of the decision-making behaviour. The management of competitors would like to know this as well; in particular, they need to understand the history of the actions of each market participant in the decision-making process. The play of a firm consists of a detailed description of its activities in carrying out its move. This is discussed in Chapter 9 through the reaction functions. If A and B progress to a price war, for example, their play would be a description of their actions. A more intriguing question is how they made the decision to engage in a price war.

It is by knowing when and how to make a decision for each player that a description may be forthcoming. Rivals will do everything to keep one another guessing. Viewing management as participants in a game is nothing new. However, in this book, we approach management as participants from a different angle by introducing the significance of type in understanding their behaviour and strategy in product and service markets, as well as in the local, national and global markets. The focus on type is key to understanding actual, observable behaviour. The behaviour translates into a conflict of subjective outcomes in a non-cooperative market where management — as individuals — compete against each other for market share; however, they keep each other guessing on their next action.

Key Decision Makers: Decision Quantum

In Chapter 1, we discussed the trade-off between two variables X and Y. A random observer can rationalise the trade-off with knowledge of the third variable, Z. However, there is nothing inevitable about the trade-off of more X for less Y. The game could have evolved differently and the key decision-maker might have chosen less X for more Y. In other words, as a player in the game the key decision-maker has no free will in the choice of X over Y. It is *enveloped* by the game and there is nothing inevitable or deterministic (always less X or always more Y) about the trade-off between X and Y.

The interplay of casual factors in a modern company or organisation — as a player in a game — is so complicated that it is impossible to predict choice without any information on player type. That a player is going to act in one way — and one way only — is not inevitable, but it is predictable within the quantum of decisions. Therefore, we label the decision-maker as the decision quantum, DQ.

The blending of management type and player type creates a DQ: the individual or group of individuals who make decisions or take action, or both. The blending is supported by CV. The earliest models of oligopolistic behaviour had assumed that firms formed expectations about the reactions (or variations) of other firms, called CVs. The

Table 7.1
Game Theory Types

	CV = 0 Expect no reaction Surprise	CV ≠ 0 Expect reaction No surprise
Price variable Price signals	Bertrand type	Stackelberg type
Non-price variables R&D expenditure, advertising	Cournot type	Chamberlin-Porterian type

Cournot, Bertrand and Stackelberg models can be interpreted as CV types (see Table 7.1).

The DQ is composed of management type and firm as they morph into one game-playing entity: the player. If a player *per se* finds itself in a market with fewer than five competitors, it behoves management to identify each rival as a type of player. At its simplest, all players are incumbents in the smallest bounded market and any new player wishing to enter that market is an entrant type. Post-entry, the entrant type evolves into an incumbent type and the blending of management type with entrant-turned-incumbent player type begins to unfold. The player is an extant (still existing) type. This becomes more acute in a market where the number of players is less than five and interdependence — the quintessence of oligopoly — is a key driver of competitor reaction. For example, both Sony and Nintendo are extant players in the video games market but Sega is not, while Microsoft has morphed from an entrant type in 2000 to an incumbent type today.

If DQ1 has a CV = 0, DQ1 does not expect a reaction from DQ2; conversely, if DQ1 has a CV ≠ 0, DQ1 anticipates a reaction from DQ2 and formulates a reply strategy (see Table 7.2). The reason why a reaction is anticipated may be due to the management's reading of the signals from the type of management blended with the player type that has become DQ2. For example, if DQ2 was characterised by DQ1 as an extant player, there is less likelihood that DQ2 would follow a price reduction by DQ1 than if DQ2 was characterised as an entrant type.

Table 7.2
Reply Strategy

	Type of management	Signal
CV = 0	Bounded rational Penrose effect	Not in a game No reply strategy
CV ≠ 0	Player Pattern recognition	Reply strategy in a game

Our treatment here is concerned with management who act only as DQs rather than as individuals: each DQ attempts to predict the actions of other DQs but does not cooperate explicitly with them. It is about management team interaction. It assumes no cooperation, but the outcome may sometimes be interpreted as implicit cooperation between DQs. Take the example of DQ1 reducing price with a CV ≠ 0; DQ2 follows with CV ≠ 0 and when DQ1 replies with a price reduction, a price war ensues. Baumol type players — such as DQ1 — who adopt a binary approach will ask themselves: Will DQ2 reduce price? Yes or No? If the answer is yes, DQ1 should anticipate a price reduction.

It is useful to address the issue of risk on the premise that DQ management are risk-averse, but being risk-averse does not preclude the taking of risks. In game strategy, there is a burden of loss in the interpretation of strategy in playing the game with rival management. Otherwise, the interpretation of risk falls back on the issue of whether it is judicious for management to play the game. Indeed, it may be the case that management opt not to play or the understanding of type is wholly inappropriate for some managements and their respective firms. The latter could define management who, in effect, increase volume in order to maximise sales revenue, cut prices and largely ignore the presence of other firms. It may be a Baumol type.

The management philosophy known as *kaizen* has captured the attention of management over the past 30 years. It is a generic term that incorporates numerous management techniques promising increased productivity and a reduction in inventories, errors and lead times with radical realignment in production technology. Described by Imai (1986) as "the basic philosophical underpinning for the best in Japanese management", *kaizen* has emerged as a process-oriented, customer-driven strategy for corporate success since 1986. It has given management the capability to quickly adopt and adapt their manufacturing processes to changing customer and market requirements. Management terms such as TQM, JIT, *kamban* and the 5-S programme are process-oriented concepts.

Poka-yoke and the nth Root

There is a lesser-known term that goes to the heart of our discussion on type and strategy: mistake-proofing or 'poka-yoke'. It is useful as a concept in understanding management type and risk (see Table 7.3). Management are risk-averse by nature, but being so does not preclude the taking of risks. Indeed, the risk — however it is quantified — has an opportunity cost of real resources and management must balance that cost with possible gains from, say, launching a new product, exciting an episodic price war or relocating a plant. The risk element is interpreted in terms of management who, as a player, finally adopts a contingency plan to complement the motive that is driving their action. The strategy adopted is observed by competitors as an action. For example, the decision to launch a new product is a binary choice: launch or delay the product. Either way, the compet-

Table 7.3
Poka-yoke = Minimise Exposure to Loss

	Make a decision	Take an action
Knowing that	No error in the game No surprise signal	Poka-yoke Moon-shot is credible
Knowing how **Knowing when**	Poka-yoke Gain second mover advantage	No error in the game No surprise Nash reply

itor can interpret the action and infer the type of management. If the expected return for not launching the product, $E(r_A)$, is greater than the expected return for launching it, $E(r_B)$, management take the risk and delay or park the product launch at this juncture in the game.

To understand this, we need to realise that $E(r_A)$ is computed as the nth root of the different risks perceived by the player. If a player decides not to launch a product, the opportunity cost of lost revenue is a risk, r_1, that must be balanced against the opportunity cost of resources devoted to producing a product that might fail, r_2, resources that could be used elsewhere in the firm, r_3, or in R&D expenditure on a different type of product, r_4. An additional factor in computing this risk is the likely reaction of a competitor. If a player, for example, adopts strategy 1 (S_1), we associate it with a risk, r_1. In order to integrate poka-yoke into this strategy, we need to associate it with a row vector of risks, $\mathbf{R}$, such that $R = (r_1, r_2, \dots r_n)$. For each r_i, there is an expected return, $E(r_i)$. To ensure mistake-proofing, management who adopt a poka-yoke position compute the nth root $\sqrt{\{E(r_1) + E(r_2) + E(r_3) + \dots + E(r_n)\}}$. The action, S_1, is contingent on r_1 with an nth root expected return. Across the strategy set, $\mathbf{S}$, there are S_1 to S_n; the strategy with the maximum return computed using the nth root formula is the adopted strategy. The choice is binary, that is, management as a player will choose from a set of strategies and can refer back to historic $E(r)$ for any related strategy.

Burden of Loss Standard

The complexity of the strategy set mirrors that of playing the game; there is a **burden of loss** standard that impinges on management in adopting mistake-proofing or 'poka-yoke'. In other words, it requires management to minimise the firm's exposure to loss. In many respects, the interpretation of strategy takes place in the context of playing the game with rival management, while the interpretation of risk tackles the issue of whether it is judicious for management to do so. As noted, it may be the case that management decide not to play a game *per se*, but to proceed with business. Whether this happens depends on management type, technology and time. In a world where management can influence rivals' actions by their type, a reliance on profit maximisation or shareholder value as the key driver of management behaviour may no longer seem reasonable. Making a decision, and knowing that it has to be made, is crucial.

In oligopoly markets, management find themselves closer to the rhythm and pattern of real price movements. Prices are no longer arbitrarily guided by a march towards the Holy Grail of a perfectly competitive price. Instead, prices fall into a pattern that pervades the market for products and management must redeem themselves through their behaviour in the firm. Management's rational nature can help them decide to accept the reality or to change the pattern of observed behaviour through their own actions and reactions in the market. The economic price standards appear arbitrary or are imposed by institutions without any reference to the right reason or the preferences of management. There are price opposites of the perfectly competitive equilibrium, such as a cartel-like price, which can be turned into a negative signal (quaternity) when included with monopoly and dominant positions. In this view of the business world, DQ management — robbed of their rationality — must avoid a cartel price or monopoly position. Otherwise, their behaviour will be constrained and retarded by external factors.

Strategy Set

A fact finder may observe play in a market by observing management actions; for management, the situation is more complex. Observed behaviour may not be repeated or, as in our fictitious example, player A may not have expected a reaction from player B because in the past the latter did not react. This is a crucial point in understanding the relevance of management type to a meaningful and pragmatic definition of strategy. Management make decisions every day, many of which are internal, organisational-type decisions pertaining to budgeting, personnel or finance. The how and when of those decisions, the taking of actions, are generally confined within the organisation.

If we return to our fictitious example, player A may not have expected a reaction from player B because in the past B did not react. Hence, A observed a pattern of behaviour and did not have a reply. The converse is equally important: Why did B react? What was it about B that made it deviate from past behaviour? We will examine a few explanations in terms of type of management, zero-sum constraint, market systems, market share consolidation and innovation (see Table 7.4). Each of them provides a template that overhangs the strategy set.

The nub of the issue is this: When the taking of an action spills over into the market, it inevitably leads to a reaction from a rival. The identity of the rival may be unknown or the reaction of a particular rival may be unexpected. It is not every day that management must take an action that triggers off a likely reaction from a near-rival in a market. Likewise, they do not need to take an action that requires knowledge of the likely reactions from near-rivals in a competitive market. Doing nothing at this juncture translates into not making any decision and may be observed as such by the near-rival.

Today, for the majority of companies, the management team has to evaluate the risks associated with market participation. They can integrate and adopt mistake-proofing or a 'poka-yoke' into their

Table 7.4
Blended Management

Type of player A is determined by:	Firm A = player A	Firm A ≠ player A
Zero-sum interdependence	Yes	No
Market system	Yes	No
Market consolidation	Yes n < 5	No n > 5
Innovation and time	Yes	Yes
Type of management	Vertical blending	No blending

decision making: management evaluate the risks, decide to play the game, become players and adopt strategies accordingly.

The important element is that management are risk-averse. This implies that they evaluate the risks, take the risk that will yield the greatest expected return and enter the market as strategic players. Non-participation or admission that strategic behaviour is inapplicable to one's firm is — in and of itself — a strategic decision, regardless of whether the management wish to concede that point to rival participants. It is the nature of the market-as-a-game that another firm will interpret this decision strategically; it may signal, for example, old traditional management styles, a possibility of poaching market share or a lack of R&D expenditures. The management who opt not to participate must bear some responsibility for that decision should the firm be left exposed to the vagaries of strategic game play and is forced to play catch-up in a rapidly changing business world. This approximates the concept of short-termism and best characterises a type traditionally referred to as 'risk-averse management'.

Minimise Errors

The importance of poka-yoke is to minimise errors by identifying a mistake. Ellsberg (1961) has shown that individuals prefer bets with known probabilities to those with unknown probabilities. In order to minimise the opportunity cost in any trade-off between variables X and Y, management have a third variable, Z. They are prepared to trade different pairs of X and Y provided Z remains constant in time period t and increases in time period $t+1$. Pairs of X and Y for all n variables, $(X1,Y1)$ ... (Xn,Yn), translate into a business strategy: **more** profits and **less** revenues, or **less** costs and **more** profits. A business strategy requires action. Rational management prefer strategies that yield higher values for Z and are indifferent to those that produce equal values. If management can realise a higher value of Z by lowering costs in time period t, the strategy observed will be a lowering of costs. Keeping to type affords management a degree of certainty, as well as a probability that the trade-off between X and Y will deliver a Z-result.

The Z-result is like a default outcome, which allows management to overcome the Penrose effect. Consequently, the Z-result is intricately linked to management type. The CEO is type Z. If player A chooses Z (maximise value) **more often**, that is, with a higher probability than Z (maximise revenues), he will be seen as attaching a **higher utility** to it (Harsanyi, 1977). In Framework T/3, there are a range of financial candidates or variables for X, Y and Z. While the list is not exhaustive, these include revenue, price, profits, costs, R&D expenditure, dividends, value and profitability. There is also management utility, U, which is a measure of satisfaction and a key driver of managerial models. However, it is not true utility as described in the neoclassical paradigm. As defined by Gul and Pesendorfer (2007), management utility is a **choice utility**. A determinant of behaviour, it explains why management opt to maximise growth, value or total revenue.

In other words, personal satisfaction is derived by management in the realisation of an objective. In Figure 7.1, the pay-off in strategy A (action A) is greater than that in strategy B (action B) if the non-zero CV is correct. Management are not surprised by the reaction of a competitor. Although it is critical to identify competitors, the near rival — that competitor who has the greatest probability

Figure 7.1
Nash Premise

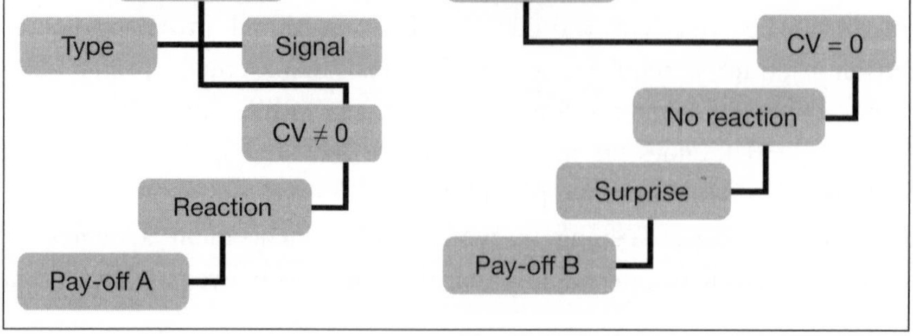

of being the first to react to one's action — is the main competitor. Hence, in a business framework described by technology and time, the identity of the nearest rival becomes more critical and more difficult in the absence of an understanding of player type. The first response is to construct a CTL of competitor signals over a period of time.

Noise

In a market, noise is a distraction. McCullough (2008) describes noise in a game in terms of an error "when you might accidentally defect when you mean to cooperate or your partner will read your genuine cooperation as a defection." In Framework T/3, noise is a signal to get players to think X-way, do Y-way. When a player is in decline in time period t because of increased competition and shrinking demand, noise will exist in the market-as-a-game. In other words, one player may think X but do and signal Y. When the rival reacts to Y, believing that the latter is the opponent's true choice, the opponent plays X. As defined in Figure 7.2, noise is a signal and may manifest itself in a game when a player is playing not to lose rather than win.

In the case of Nokia, noise captures the company's push into mobile services with Ovi in early 2007, as illustrated in the CTL in Figure 7.3. Ovi was launched in early 2009 as Ovi Maps and Ovi Mail, and was described in technology magazines as "a hub that integrates mobile services between handsets and PCs" (*The Economist*, 6 December 2008). In 2009, Apple Inc launched iPhone 3GS (see Figure 7.4 on page 115).

Figure 7.2
Signal Shower

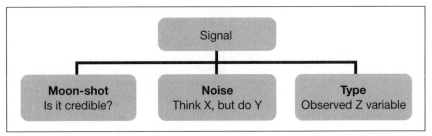

Figure 7.3
Critical Timeline — Apple *vs* Nokia, 2005 to 2008

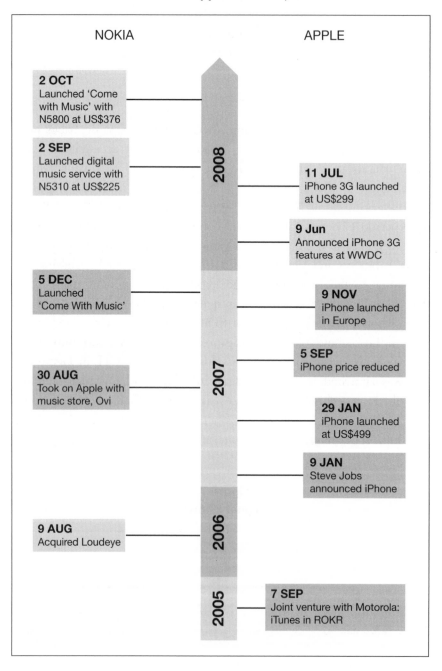

In 2007, Nokia had a reputed worldwide market share of 40 per cent in handsets before the launch of the iPhone. In order to protect that market share — so that it does not fall, say, to 30 per cent — Nokia was creating noise by signalling a strategy that focuses not on growth of handsets *per se*, but on the services it provides.

In the 1990s, Motorola's introduction of a mobile phone with a clamshell design may well have been noise in the emerging game of vying for dominance in the handset market.

Noise in a Tumbling Price

In the market for mobile phones, price and non-price characteristics are important in the game. Price falls can signal a Baumol type. If players believe there is a Baumol type in a game, price should not fall below the trigger price because net total revenue accruing to any player would fall. A rival, observing no price fall, believes that no player is a Baumol type. Hence, no player reduces price and none of them knows that there is a Baumol type. Consequently, no player moves to reduce price. This is a paradox.

If a player knows that the rival **believes** the former is not a Baumol type, price will not be increased above the trigger price as the net total revenue accruing to the player would fall. Consequently, it is only when the player **knows** that the rival realises it is a Baumol type that the player will reduce price. Ultimately, it is the action of reducing price (if present price is above the trigger price) that reveals the true identity of the player as a Baumol type.

In the elastic range, a high prevailing price can be maintained to maximise profits in a market with five or fewer players. An action by a Baumol player to reduce price — in order to recoup lost revenues — should be signalled by that player as a one-shot move. A one-shot move is unlikely to provoke a price reaction from a rival if the latter knows it as such and can observe the price falling to the Baumol player's trigger price.

Yet, if no player reduces price, prices will not tumble. For example, Apple and Samsung could succumb to this paradox of a tumbling price; as price falls in order to compete, the trigger price — activated by changing consumer preferences for more functionalities — embeds a sequentially lower bound on the market price. As the game unfolds, the market price could fall to zero. The Nokia N97, for example, was launched in the United Kingdom in October 2009 at zero price. As that happens, a greater demand for functionalities creates an inelastic demand that would warrant a price increase in time. The identification of patterns in observed signals is necessary for each player to isolate a rival's strategy as a string of price moves across the CTL. It is imperative that patterns are identified in the market-as-a-game where innovation, rapid product development, technology and demand for functionalities define the game dimension.

The significance of technology is reflected in the CTL for Apple *versus* RIM in 2009 (see Figure 7.4). The competing products are differentiated by functionality (2G or 3G), but not by network. The market-as-a-game exhibits a range of observations, such as Sony Ericsson which target games fans with its smartphones. In a bid to distinguish itself from rival mobile firms, Sony Ericsson used PlayStation technology in its 2009 products. Another example was the HTC Touch, which was popular in Asia because it was cheaper than the iPhone and can be used on various cellular networks.

The Mistakes of Dark Strategy

Management are used to dealing with incomplete information, and they make decisions daily out of uncertainty. Increasingly, new technology is presenting new challenges to management, and decision making is constrained by the kinetic equation

$$\frac{d\mathsf{F}}{dt} = -1.$$

Across their suite of products and services, there is at least one product or service market that is evolving into a market-as-a-game. Thus, it behoves management to play the signalling game. Dark strategy facilitates mistake-roofing in the market-as-a-game which management already believe in; the critical issue is the observed action of a competitor.

Figure 7.4
Critical Timeline — Apple *vs* RIM, 2007 to 2009

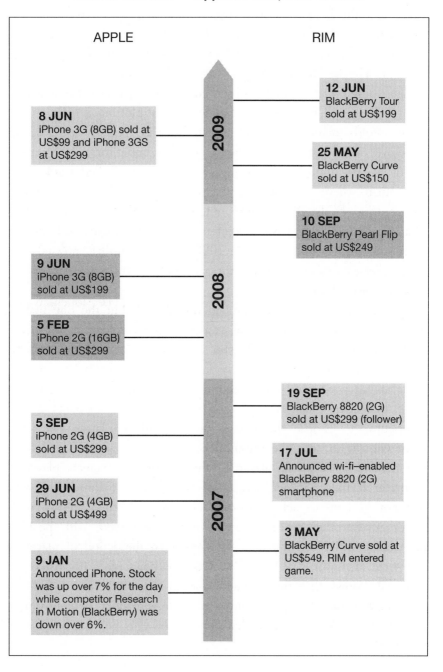

Strategy is a string of moves. Dark strategy refers to how management act after having observed the moves of a competitor while being aware that the latter not only observes the action as a reaction, but also knows that management are observing them. The sequence of observed moves can be plotted as a CTL and illustrated in Figures 7.3 and 7.4. The key to unlocking a sustainable competitive advantage is to determine a pattern in the observed moves, a pattern that management believe will be repeated if they act. By plotting a CTL as the game unfolds, management will see an emerging pattern and a string of moves that define the strategy of a competitor. Management could also use the pattern to engage in a process called **backward induction** where they plot — based on their belief system about competitors — the likely future outcome should they act now. It is what Apple Inc could have predicted in 2007 (in Figure 7.4) as the likely reaction from Blackberry in 2008 and — with that knowledge in the market-as-a-game — played the game differently in 2007 to obtain a competitive advantage.

There are many competitors in the market, but the one that is likely to react first in the market-as-a-game is referred to as the near-rival competitor. Management who adopt dark strategy are **secure** in the market-as-a-game. Security in Framework T/3 is ascribed to management who avoid the three mistakes of strategy. In a signalling game, the secure management is convinced that they can persuade the competitor to choose the correct action and the latter will trust them enough to act. The duration of the signalling cycle at $t = T$ will depend on whether player B, the competitor, expects player A to prefer it to act if signalled. A near rival is that competitor who will not hesitate to act if its only alternative is to acquiesce with player A. In other words, a near rival is one who, with positive probability, will react first at $t = K < T$ to the action of player A at $t = K$. However, if at $t = K < T$ competitor C does not react and player A knows that the former is aware that its reaction will **at least** lead to tumbling prices and a possible zero-price equilibrium at $t = T$, player A can assume that competitor C is not a near rival at $t = K < T$.

First Mistake: Zero-Price Outcome

The type of player that is signalled embodies some, but not all, of the decision-relevant private information. Player type is signalled by all players. It allows any player to observe a common signal in the action of a player and to retain a private signal as noise or a moon-shot.

The private signal allows management the flexibility to react. Both technology and time are significant due to the curse of differentiation created by technology and the kinetic equation

$$\frac{d\overline{F}}{dt} = -1,$$

respectively (see Chapters 1 and 2). A small but non-zero number of players of Bertrand type with $CV = 0$ proceed to reduce price in the belief that there will be no reaction from a near rival. However, there is a reaction. This is a mistake that reflects a lack of understanding of the game and could result in a zero-price equilibrium outcome. When a player makes such a mistake, it could update its belief system on hindsight. To rectify this mistake, dark strategy prescribes a solution based on the origin of management beliefs.

Second Mistake: Failed Execution

A second mistake occurs in a Stackelberg type player with a non-zero CV who fails in the execution of the strategy. The executable strategy should favour the signals more than any prior signal on observed action. In the Razr example, any reduction in price in 2004 should have discounted a 4GB iPod to US$199 at $t = T$. Management are in a Bayesian game (Vives, 2005) when the weight attached by them to prior observed actions at $t = T$ is greater than that attached to signals at $t = T$. Bayesian type management see what they want to see and ignore the signals. To correct this mistake, dark strategy prescribes a solution based on the significance of signals.

The demise of Motorola's Razr is a good example of the second mistake when its management sets its eyes on the fashionable, highly inelastic US$400 mobile phone in early 2000 ($t = K$), mass produced it and flooded the market with it at a lower price. Subsequently, sales fell sharply. In 2012, Motorola was on the ascendancy with the newly launched Motorola Razr i smartphone. Now embedded in Google, we await the signalled launch of Google's new Moto X smartphone in October 2013. For further discussion on Google's signals, see the section on *yellow snowflakes* in Chapter 10.

Third Mistake: Lagged Differentiation

The third mistake of dark strategy occurs when management adopt new technology or product functionalities at time period t = K < T and rush to mass produce at t = T and the product fails, or the firm experiences excess capacity at t = T when consumers baulk at the new product and sales fall below optimal production levels.

Consumers have time-dependent preferences: they do not know what they want at t = T, but if it is available at time period t = K < T they will buy it in insignificant numbers until the technology has gained an externality in use. To amend this mistake, dark strategy prescribes a solution based on playing a game not to lose (second mover advantage) rather than to win. With X per cent market share at t = K < T, a player plays not to lose in order to avoid (X − 1)% at t = T. Management, too, often play to win (X + 1)% at t = K < T, but end up with (X − 1)%.

The Nash Trap

We can better satisfy our appetites in an oblique manner, than by their headlong and impetuous motion.
—**David Hume**

T he central contribution of game theory to the economics of strategic management is the introduction of a new language in understanding how to formulate and study strategic or intercompany optimisation involving two or more players. There is a wealth of applications in the literature, but we suggest that there are two fundamentally different classes of application of game theory to economic problems in business. The first is the application of two-person zero-sum games to tactical business problems. The second is the application of n-person non-constant-sum-games to strategic issues involving threat analysis and price wars. It is this combination that provides the genesis of the economics of strategy.

When our interests are confined to applications of the two-person zero-sum game, a reasonably strong case can be made for management as *homo ludens* (game-playing man) — an intelligent, calculating entity with no personality or psychological foibles — playing against an equally bloodless opponent. We can extend the concept of individual rational behaviour to the two-person zero-sum game. When our concerns are strategic and the game is one of non-zero mixed-motives optimisation — there is neither coincidence nor opposition of interests — the model of an individual actor may not suffice to capture the behaviour of the players. It is in this context that we have introduced the idea of a decision quantum to help differentiate between management as an individual and the management team working as a group, as well as the different groups functioning as a product market. A host of assumptions concerning the players and their game environment are introduced in Chapter 9 to provide a model of business reality for analysis.

Game-playing Man

Many years have passed since the publication of the seminal work on the theory of games by Nash (1950), Schelling (1960) and Shubik (1960). Each of them had questioned the application of game theory and gamesmanship to strategic analysis. The study and formulation of the principles of war date back to the writings of Sun Tzu *circa* 500 BC. Although the seeds were sown thousands of years ago, the development of a mathematical language in the study of conflict, cooperation and negotiation did not occur until the advent of the theory of games.

Notwithstanding the market structure, what is important to management is the degree of entry and their belief system on entrant types. Efficient entry is also best understood within the parameters of the type of competition that prevail in a market, including combat competition, scramble competition and contest competition (McNutt, 2005). It is best characterised by an efficient entry price, which is a long-run equilibrium price of entry.

Market Systems

Whether players in a market cooperate and lock themselves into binding commitments — which may be caught by antitrust legislation — depends on the rules of conduct for player behaviour in that market. McNutt has argued that there is a Boolean network of player behaviour — the rule stipulates that each player acts on price only if two other players act. Player A makes a decision if two other players have done so, but each player can decide whether to act at each decision point. In many respects, it is about aggressive competition. Under scramble competition, for example, the market is evenly divided and the effects of competition are the same for all competitors. Scramble may manifest as changes in the size or number of players. Combat competition is characteristic of stable markets where the acquisition of market share requires constant defence by the incumbent types.

If the market-as-a-game is played just once, allow for a unique pay-off of (2,2). It can be any number, but both players receive exactly the same amount. Each player knows exactly what they want to do (they have a dominant strategy) and each has the easiest of decisions to face — keep prices high and receive 2. Both players prefer to be in the top left cell of the matrix in Table 8.1 because in four cycles of this game, a player could receive a pay-off of

Table 8.1
Prisoners' Dilemma

	A: High price	A: Low price
B: High price	2,2	0,3
B: Low price	3,0	1,1

$8 = 2+2+2+2$. However, player A has a dominant strategy of competing to a low price and trying to do better by obtaining a pay-off of 3, but 3 can be obtained only when player B continues to keep its prices high.

In other words, if B keeps prices high, it is because he trusts A to do likewise and *vice versa*. Thus, B trusts A; but A, knowing that, betrays B. When player B realises that player A has lowered its price, it follows and both find themselves in the lower right cell of the matrix with a pay-off of (1,1). A cartel between A and B might seem a solution, but with an inherent incentive to cheat or betray, enforcement of the cooperative solution might prove difficult, *vide* the arguments in McNutt (2005). Cartels may not last very long. If one player believes that the other player will always cooperate and keep prices high, there is an incentive to betray or cheat. The issue is trust: If B keeps its prices high, can it really trust A to do the same? Collectively, both players face a dilemma: How do they obtain the cooperative outcome of 8 rather than the non-cooperative outcome of 7 or 4? Player A now ends up with $7 = 2+3+1+1$ or $4 = 1+1+1+1$ if B punishes it for the betrayal by always keeping prices low. This is a recognised **punishment strategy**, signalling to A the pay-off 4 in time period t+1 instead of 8. In trying to do better, one can end up worse off! David Hume, a Scottish philosopher writing in the 18th century, captured the idea: "We can better satisfy our appetites in an oblique manner, than by their headlong and impetuous motion." Remember that the future is not what it used to be!

Nash Equilibrium

In the exchange of prices, players interact with each other by using prices as signals. An incumbent and an entrant, or two incumbents, can face classic coordination problems. Conflicts can arise. In a two-person game, a pair of strategies will form a Nash equilibrium when each player cannot do better given the strategy the other player has adopted. A **Nash equilibrium** is a pair of strategies such that each is a best response to the other. The pay-off $(1,1)$ in Table 8.1 is an example of a Nash equilibrium. To test whether a strategy combination forms a Nash equilibrium, consider the following: let us call the strategy of the first player x* and the strategy of the second player y*. In a Nash equilibrium, the equilibrium strategies are played with certainty or with a probability of 1. When the Nash equilibrium involves only strategies that are played with certainty, we have a pure strategy equilibrium. The alternative to a pure strategy equilibrium is a mixed strategy equilibrium: each player adopts a strategy that is selected at random from a number of pure strategies. This argument is one of the more difficult ones in the book. For further reading, refer to Nalebuff and Dixit (2008).

The Nash theorem states that there is a collection of strategies (the sequence of moves) such that it is not in the interest of any player to alter its strategy (Nash, 1950). What happens when two or more players change their strategies? If the players chat before the game to coordinate their strategies to obtain $(2,2)$ in Table 8.1, they *do not trust each other* and will end up at a Nash equilibrium, $(1,1)$. In retrospect, one player could have done better by using a different strategy to obtain 3. Hence, it is irrational to play a strategy that one regrets afterwards. We discuss the regret strategy in greater detail in Chapter 9, but for now the only agreement possible for the players — which none of them will regret afterwards — is on the choice of a Nash equilibrium point. McNutt (2005) has discussed this scenario in terms of a semi-ordering of prices, where x* corresponds to a 'reduced' price by a defendant-firm and y* corresponds to a 'lower' price for an entrant-plaintiff. The pair (x*, y*) is called aggressive pricing (see Figure 10.3 on page 175).

First Hurdle Initiative

When we raise the question of solution to a game, interesting issues arise between two-player games and n-person games. Dynamic games with few players, for example, have a leading contender in the perfect equilibrium, but it is not unique. For tactical problems involving two players, the saddle point or maximin-minimax solution provides a reasonable solution to a two-person game. Strategic problems have been considered primarily as games in extensive, strategic or coalitional form. Taking the first step in a game is crucial for management: If they take the first step and rivals follow, they assume the mantle of leader. A volunteer is needed, but both players realise that if both of them volunteer the worst possible outcome will obtain.

Both players have an incentive to volunteer given that the other player does not. Because of this incentive, it can be argued the precondition that the other player does not volunteer may not hold. Hence, volunteering becomes the optimal strategy. The dilemma here is that it cannot be optimal for both players simultaneously, that is, the players do not have dominant strategies.

Unlike the Prisoners' Dilemma where there is a unique Nash equilibrium, the solution in the Volunteer's Dilemma can be characterised by either one of the Nash equilibria (2,3) or (3,2). In the Volunteers' Dilemma (see Table 8.2), no strategy is available for one player to punish the other player for deviating from a quasi-cooperative path.

Table 8.2
Volunteers' Dilemma

	S3	S4
S1	(2,2)	(2,3)
S2	(3,2)	(1,1)

Classic Prisoners' Dilemma

Earlier in this chapter, we represented the possible outcomes to demonstrate the maxim of one player seeking to do better than (2,2) by obtaining a 3 but ending up at (1,1). The player can obtain 3 only if the other player receives zero. In other words, one player opts for a low price only when the second player keeps its price high. That is the only way to secure a 3. However, the second player soon realises that zero is an outcome and reduces its price. Hence, both players end up at (1,1).

The only solution is communication, and this is illegal in the real world due to the antitrust legislation against cartels and price fixing. In other words, one player — a price leader — initiates an agreement to remain at the (2,2) outcome. In many markets, a fact finder would observe constant or fixed prices. However, mere adherence to a fixed price is not sufficient evidence of belonging to a cartel. There must be evidence of a rule or mechanism to ensure that the (2,2) outcome obtains across all periods and there is no incentive to cheat because of, say, a punishment strategy.

If both players in Table 8.3 communicate over a four-period game, the total pay-offs amount to $2+2+2+2 = 8$. If one player deviates from the agreement and cheats by charging a low price in the second period, it obtains $2+3 = 5$. However, the other player observes the cheating behaviour and reduces its price. It does not punish the first player who

Table 8.3
Classic Prisoners' Dilemma

	High price	Low price
High price	(2,2) We can both have a 2 pay-off.	(0,3) You want this 3 pay-off instead.
Low price	(3,0)	(1,1) We both end up with a 1 pay-off.

now obtains $2+3+1+1 = 7$ with a realisation of $1+1+1+1 = 4$ for all periods, unless there is an agreement not to cheat. This is difficult to maintain in the real world unless a credible punishment mechanism can be put in place by one of the players. Today, enforcement agencies rely on whistle-blower legislation to entice a cartel member to expose the cartel mechanism. Instability is built into the game when external incentives from a third party to do better are provided to a player. It is rational to betray and cheat in a cooperative game, *vide* the discussion on the Prisoners' Dilemma later in the chapter.

Folk Theorem

In game theory, the Folk Theorem spells out the means by which firms can attain outcomes that appear collusive without necessarily engaging in overt collusion — or even discussing together what to do. It shows how collusive outcomes can be attained 'as (sub-game perfect) non-cooperative equilibria' (Friedman, 2000). However, in producing cooperative behaviour from a conventional non-cooperative equilibrium, it has been argued that the Folk Theorem blurs the distinction between explicit collusion and tacit collusion. From the standpoint of intent, this renders antitrust investigation a delicate matter. In addition, it raises the possibility of partial collusion where players collude on certain choices (prices) and not on others (location or markets), as argued by Friedman, Jehiel and Thisse (1995). It also leads to unintentional cooperation or an asymmetric sameness in price standard discussed in McNutt (2005) and later in this book.

Mixed Strategy

A mixed strategy arises when one player randomly decides to change — or not change — price with equal probability. In a predatory pricing game, this strategy may not be part of a Nash equilibrium. A national competition agency or court, for example, would need to discover the other firm's response to this strategy. The other firm would compute the expected pay-offs from each of the pure strategies that would accrue from changing and not changing price. The agency or court must then determine whether management are acting rationally if they choose a strategy that does not maximise the firms' pay-off. Alternatively, the agency or court must balance this with whether the management of an incumbent firm are willing to predate in order to convince entrants that they are aggressive rather than rational.

In the application to strategic business decisions, what is equally important for management is to understand the game. The strategy may well depend on management's interpretation of the context in which they obtained the move or took the action. This is a classic dilemma in cartel pricing: If player 1 keeps prices high, both players obtain (2,2) in Table 8.3 and the game is over. If player 1 is the leader, its signal to keep prices high will sustain the cartel. Both players trust each other. However, if player 2 misreads the signal or opts to lower the price, its move will end the trust game at a new lower pay-off. Player 1 may punish player 2. The latter's strategy will depend on the context in which the move was obtained.

Making decisions and taking actions can only be understood with reference to the subjective behaviour of management. Hence, it is useful to interpret decision making by differentiating between knowing that (making a decision) and knowing how and when to act (taking an action). The iconic Prisoners' Dilemma arises in games precisely because one player takes an action to break away from the agreed decision at this point in time by presuming that the other player will not react. Paradoxically, while management may prefer to avoid conflict, individually they may prefer an outcome that can be obtained only through conflict. This is the conundrum embedded in the Prisoners' Dilemma and expressed as follows: In trying to do better than the status quo by taking an action, the individual ends up worse off. Nevertheless, someone must take the first step; otherwise, there is no game and there will be no market interaction.

Morphing into a Decision Quantum

An understanding of type allows management — as a player in a game — to minimise the trial-and-error learning process whereby they gradually discover that only some strategies work. At time period t, management do not have complete knowledge of details of the game. The market in which they are competing evolves into either a combat system, a contest system or a scramble system (McNutt, 2005). Consequently, management as an individual evolves in the market-as-a-game.

As they recognise the degree of interdependence, management type morphs into a decision quantum (DQ) — a player — and the rules of the game, type of players and pay-offs become common knowledge. Nokia's completion of the purchase of Symbian in 2008 is an interesting example of management type morphing into a DQ. A signal to Apple, Google and Microsoft was sent in the summer of 2008 when Nokia completed the deal to buy out Symbian, the leading maker of operating system software for mobile phones. The software is used in at least 50 per cent of mobile phones and plays an integral role in mobile music and photo sharing. The mobile market is evolving into services and players must ask: Will one operating system dominate in the handset market, much like Microsoft Windows does in the PC market? Much will depend on the game dimension; on rival players such as Google's Android, BlackBerry, iPhone and Linux; and on the need for handset manufacturers to sign up for one software.

SMIN

An engineering solution would change the rules of the game. Let us coin a new word and call a new 'want-to-have' product the 'small and thin (SMIN)'. This can combine the functionalities of a smartphone with those of a netbook and it could offer a first-mover advantage to any player who launches it first to the market. However, if the new product resembles a netbook, it may not fit neatly into the jacket pocket or purse; if it resembles a smartphone, it may have limited processing power or the screen may be too small to facilitate word processing. Whatever the dislike, consumers will not buy the product if it does not match their specific set of functionalities. Thus, many players are prepared to wait and secure a second-mover advantage. In the interim, there is a risk that an unknown or smaller player might just get it right and capture that elusive first-mover advantage. However, that is a judgement call for management to make as a DQ, and Framework T/3 complements the existing strategic toolbox deployed by management in making that call.

In 2009, Dell launched the Adamo (initially in China), Celio's Redfly C8N received mixed reviews after its launch, Acer displayed the M900 smartphone and Nokia signalled its entry into the laptop market. For SMIN devices, the market-as-a-game represents an interesting example of an evolving market system in mobile devices. PC players and mobile phone players do see an opportunity, but are cautious. There is history in the market-as-a-game from the 1990s when Apple's Newton PDA, Dell's MP3 player and HP's line of televisions failed as products. Consumers with time-dependent preferences and changing demand for mobile devices are creating a challenge for the players in this market-as-a-game. An engineering solution may exist and potentially offer a DQ player the first-mover advantage. Mistakes can be costly. However, with changing demand and ever-changing new technology, mistake proofing is mandatory in order to at least predict the reaction of competitors and to prepare to react to the uncertainty created by type, technology and time.

The 'Nash Trap': Always Best to Confess

To understand game theory is to understand the delicate balance of the Nash trap: My friend and I are thieves and we have just been caught by the police, but the prosecutor has enough evidence to put us away for five years for carrying a concealed weapon rather than a maximum of ten years for the robberies.

As long as we cooperate and do not confess, we will get a year in prison. The prosecutor comes to my cell and points out that if my friend pleads guilty and I do not, he will receive a reduced sentence for pleading guilty but I will get a maximum of ten years. I know that I can do better than a year in prison by striking a deal with the prosecutor, but do worse when both of us end up with a (−5) if we plead guilty at the same time (see Table 8.4). Hence, both will be worse off. I am better off confessing; we are both better off by not confessing. One way to escape the Nash trap is to signal your intent to cooperate or engage in bargaining.

Table 8.4
Nash Trap

	Do not confess Plead not guilty	Confess Plead guilty
Do not confess Plead not guilty	–1,–1	–10,0 (go free)
Confess Plead guilty	0 (go free),–10	–5,–5

Hypothesis: 'I think you think I think'

The true state in a game occurs when you think like your opponent; if you do not think like your opponent, you would put too much emphasis on the pay-off corresponding to the true state instead of treating all states equally. This is called the curse of knowledge. In decoding strategy, it is of interest to management to know not only about behaviour, but about other minds as well. A theory of other minds would come in handy for any business person.

Dennett (1996) points out that an animal does not need to consult any internal model of the mind to anticipate behaviour. It could just be equipped with a large list of **if-then** contingencies. He advocates that all individuals (in all species) learn through evolution; a surprising number of species find themselves compelled to learn in a second way — what he referred to as conditioned learning — and some select species are pressured to learn in a third way by using information of the mind. Here, we have consciousness and — as the philosopher Karl Popper puts it — "permits our hypotheses to die in our stead" (Dennett, 1996).

In *The Singing Gorilla*, Page (1999, page 189) observes a hungry lioness — hunkered behind a mound — considering a grazing buffalo 30 meters away. A buffalo is no wildebeest. It is one of the most aggressive and dangerous animals in Africa. The lioness understands this. Yes, she is hungry, and so are her cubs; but no, she is not that hungry and not that good a mother. She will let her hypothesis die in its stead. She strolls away.

Sub-game: g ⊂ G

A player has incomplete information on type; it is not always possible to know the opponent's type. Type is based on actions observed as signals in the game, such as reducing price, entering a market or launching a new product or service after an initial move by an opponent. The action leads to an observed reaction in a game in the time continuum, that is, player A moves first in a sequence of moves and player B reacts in time. However, if player A reacts in time to a move by player B, a sub-game is observed.

A game, G, and sub-game, g ⊂ G, can occur in parallel. In this scenario, the players have imperfect information on how the game is played. In both cases, the players are bounded rationally, the Penrose effect is triggered and more intelligence gathering on type — coupled with more actions filtered into information cones — will support a degree of probability on likely reaction.

Prisoners' Dilemma

The classic representation of the Prisoners' Dilemma is that strategy 'confess' is a dominant strategy (2,2) for both players — no matter what one player does (regardless of another player's move), a better choice for the other player is to confess. Taylor and Pacelli (2008, page 118) identified an intuitive response: 'I wish I knew what my partner is doing.' They argued that this is wrong because what your partner is doing is irrelevant: you should confess.

Case 1

Player B chooses Silent. In this case, player A's choice of Confess yields an outcome of 4 from (4,1) for A, as opposed to 3 from outcome (3,3) that would have resulted from A's choice of the strategy Silent (see Table 8.5).

Table 8.5
Silence *vs* Confession

	B: Silent	B: Confess
A: Silent	3,3	1,4
A: Confess	4,1	2,2

Case 2

Player B chooses Confess. In this case, player A's choice of Confess yields an outcome of 2 from (2,2) for A, as opposed to 1 from outcome (1,4) that would have resulted from A's choice of the strategy Silent (see Table 8.5).

Grim Strategy

We have shown that regardless of what player B does — Case 1 or Case 2 — the strategy Confess yields a better outcome for player A than the strategy Silent. Cooperation arises if players can infer from past behaviour that their opponent is likely to be trustworthy. In the **folk theorem**, players must be forward-looking. In each time period, there is a short-term benefit from cheating. Players refrain from cheating in order to gain future benefits. If an opponent has a reputation as a trustworthy type, a player will use the experience to determine whether they believe this reputation. Otherwise, there will be punishment in the form of **grim strategy** (Besanko *et al*, 2013).

Type is important in a game, and 'keeping to type' is the cradle that rocks strategic play in a game. Players forego short-term gains for long-term benefits. It is a form of altruism or the non-selfish behaviour observed in the animal kingdom (Page, 1999). A **Griselda type** of player withdraws from a preferred selfish move and remains silent, observes cooperation and cooperates with other players.

Market-as-a-Game

They came to the fields of joy,
The fresh turf of the Fortunate Woods ...
Here was the company of those who had suffered
Wounds fighting for the Fatherland.
—Aeneid, vi., 638, 660

T he misreading of signals is one reason for the uncertainty seen in the business world. The market is introduced in terms of the market-as-a-game focusing on the interaction of competitors as players in a product market where interdependence is seen amongst the players. We do make some assumptions. **Assumption I**, the player assumption, refers to the company or firm as a player and an understanding that it is in a game with other players. We start from the premise that firms are aware of their interdependence and management — as players — are mistake-proofing. Moves and countermoves ensue until both firms arrive at an equilibrating solution.

Market-as-a-Game

Some firms do not carry this understanding of a player as described in this book, but they do compete — and compete aggressively — with each other. As long as management never perceive their interdependence, the outcome achieved is the expected outcome and not the attainable outcome. However, in different geographic markets — whether local, national or global — where the number of players is less than five, there is a greater probability that the firms are players and the management team realise that they are in a game. This is the market known as oligopoly. **Assumption II**, the definition of game assumption, states that a group of companies realise that they are in a game when the fate of one company depends not only on its own actions, but also on the actions of the rest of the companies in the market (Binmore and Dasgupta, 1986).

From a third-party perspective, a fact finder may observe play in a market through observing management behaviour and player actions, say, from signals on price, quantity or dividends policy. It is quite a different thing to infer player types in a market from observing the behaviour of the management alone. For example, by ascribing types to the management of company X, the fact finder becomes bounded rational about the player type. The fact finder, employing the principle known as Occam's razor, ignores features of the economic theory that cannot be observed. He has limited ability to distinguish one type from another. Instead, the fact finder uses experience and easy-to-process signals to sort the problem into a small number of categories. When management realise they are in a game, camouflage may take place — deliberate attempts to confuse the opponent — and the type of management is subsumed within the type of player. Consequently, player type is more difficult to predict and observe *ex-ante* in the blending of types.

In the late 1920s, the French mathematician Emil Borel wrote a series of articles to show how games, war and economic behaviour were similar activities in that they all involved the making of strategic decisions. Borel's work gained the attention of economists, and the most significant achievement was the publication by Von Neumann and Morgenstern (1944). Both economists and mathematicians began to believe that a full-fledged theory of games could be developed to provide a much better understanding of oligopoly behaviour than that offered by traditional economic theory.

In their seminal work, Von Neumann and Morgenstern classified games into those with complete information and those with incomplete information. Competition may manifest itself in different ways, such as price competition or advertising expenditures. However, in a game we are focusing on patterns of observed behaviour. In this enriched view of a market, management embedded in a firm as a player will continue to look at prices and their patterns over a period of time; they may also look at entropy in market shares (in Chapter 10, we discuss scramble, combat and contest competitions).

Unlike formal games such as chess, bridge or poker which have a well-defined beginning and ending, it is difficult to assign a clear end-point or rest-point in most models of strategic business situations. In essence, it is the responsibility of the fact finder to establish the context in which the game is played. The behaviour of management as described must be assessed in the context of the situation at hand. **Assumption III**, an assumption of symmetry, states that any differences in the abilities of individual management must be specified within the model; otherwise, all non-specified attributes are regarded as the same. As a device for simplification, the value of this assumption is significant. For example, if we wish to apply the two-person zero-sum game to a price-revenue evaluation problem involving a task on elasticity, the assumption that opposing players are equal in all respects appears reasonable. For instance, as management they each understand the economics of the total revenue test: price increases on an inelastic demand will tend to increase net total revenues.

Minimax Strategy

Suppose we have two companies who are players in a zero-sum game. The player in **bold** is Apple Inc with its iPhone and iPad platforms, and with resources sufficient to defend only one of them. The player in *italics* is Samsung who has the resources to attack either the iPhone or the iPad platform, but not both. Suppose the iPhone is more valuable to both players. Our starting point is to assume that an attack on a defended position results in neither a gain nor a loss for either player (see Table 9.1).

Table 9.1
Zero-sum Pay-off

	iPhone 5	iPad 3
Galaxy S3	0,0	3,–3
Galaxy Tab	1,–1	0,0

The game is zero-sum. If we focus on one player and give the pay-offs to Samsung, the player in *italics*, we can obtain the pay-offs accruing to Apple. Hence, the standard presentation of the game is shown in Table 9.2.

The positive entries represent a gain for Samsung, the player in *italics*, and a loss for Apple, the player in **bold**. A negative pay-off number — there are none in this game — represents a loss for Samsung and a gain for Apple. Hence, this game favours Samsung, the player in *italics*. The question is: What is Apple's — the player in **bold** — best strategy?

Table 9.2
Player Gain

	iPhone 5	iPad 3
Galaxy S3	0	3
Galaxy Tab	1	0

Apple Inc thinks that Samsung expects it to defend the iPhone. Hence, Samsung will attack the iPad. Samsung knows that Apple will reason this way, and so assuming that Apple will defend the iPad, Samsung will attack the iPhone. Samsung plays by launching the Galaxy S4. However, Samsung also expects Apple to reason in this way. This line of reasoning suggests that some kind of game-tree analysis will reveal a strategy as Apple's best choice. But it is more complex than that — Apple must choose to play a minimax strategy that minimises the maximum amount Samsung can expect to get in the evolving game while maximising the gain Apple can expect to derive from it. Apple's minimax play is a low-priced nano iPhone.

Reasonable Belief

However, individual management, **homo sapiens**, is limited in both its ability and capability to see, comprehend, process and act on all the information available. His strategic cousin, **homo ludens**, is regarded as a simplification of management with bounded rationality. In the study of threats, bargaining and negotiations applied to management and business, the blending of type of management with type of player into a decision quantum (DQ) — the game-playing type analogue of a management team — may be worth considering. The behaviour of the DQ is said to be rational only insofar as it coincides with an equilibrating behaviour. It is reasonable as long as the player has sound judgement. Consider the pay-off matrix from the game theory literature shown in Table 9.3.

Table 9.3
Homo Ludens

	A	B
a	1,1	0,0
b	0,0	1,1

The row player can play *a* if she can reasonably believe that the column player could play A, since *a* is a best response to A. She can reasonably believe that the column player can play A if it is reasonable for the column player to believe that the row player could play *a*. He can believe that she will play *a* if it is reasonable for him to believe that she could play *a*. This provides an infinite chain of consistent beliefs that result in the players playing to an outcome (*a*, A). In business, it is critical that each player has a belief system and each action should be defined in terms of a CV (see Chapter 7). In other words, a Baumol type with CV = 0 could reduce price to increase total revenue. Unless management signal this type to the market as a player, other players might interpret this price reduction as a threat and react by reducing price. This tit for tat, as illustrated in Figure 9.4 on page 143, could continue until the signals are matched. Alternatively, a signal to the market that player X is a Baumol type will allow other players to believe that this is true and the observed price reduction will be a one-shot price move that does not require a reaction.

In Henrich (2004), for example, social preferences are included in the Prisoners' Dilemma (PD) game to allow the possibility that some players are averse to inequality. It is argued that some players in a PD game prefer the more equal — but personally less profitable — outcome of mutual cooperation to the more asymmetrical pay-off produced by defecting against a cooperator. In the PD pricing game, when a player deviates by lowering price, there is a temptation for another player to follow. In other words, there is a kind of reciprocity in pricing as follows: My rival has lowered price; would it pay for me to do the same? The reciprocal price may not be so easily forthcoming in business, as management are either increasingly subject to shareholder constraints or do not have the production capacity at a point in time to proceed with a matching price reduction.

Price Tumbles

Therefore, DQ1's perception of DQ2 will influence its decision to commit resources to either avoid or precipitate a price tumble. Consequently, the reaction system must be interpreted in such a way that the roll-out of DQ1's price — in retrospect, the history of DQ1's prices — is relevant to DQ2's action. The price reaction functions are linear and the positive slope indicates that a given price reduction from DQ1 (fixed amount of resources) is triggered off by a given price reaction from DQ2. This action-reaction is only possible over a limited period of time before each DQ begins to read the signals from the game. The essence of the competitive process lies in trying to understand the complex web of competitors' behaviour. The reaction function allows management to track the price reactions of competitors. In a game under the zero-sum constraint, management will soon learn to weigh competitors' price reaction more than the limitations imposed by demand elasticity. This is the essence of strategic pricing.

'Price war' is a term used in business to indicate a state of intense rivalry accompanied by a sequence of multi-player price reductions. One competitor will lower its price, and (in sequence) others will lower their prices to match it. If one of the reactors reduces its price below the original cut price, a new round of price reduction is initiated. Price war is usually costly in terms of the opportunity cost of real resources deployed to defend market shares. Management should avoid price wars that are costly and erode profits.

Bertrand Model

The focus here is on strategic complements in a highly differentiated oligopoly market, and on the likely price reactions in such a market. This model examines the pricing behaviour of interdependent companies

Figure 9.1
Bertrand Zero-price Solution

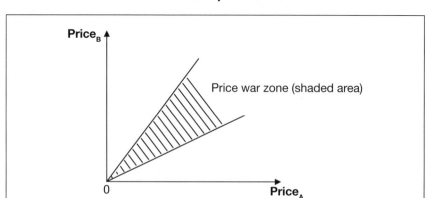

in a product market with few competitors. It is more applicable to the oligopoly markets. Figure 9.1 shows non-intersection of the reaction functions of companies A and B. The price equilibrium is zero at the origin. There is every likelihood that both players could drive the price to the (0,0) price equilibrium as the game will continue until the equilibrium price is reached.

The challenge for the Bertrand model is to explain why:

(1) in the absence of overt collusion, in some markets competing players are able to maintain high prices, such as the US cigarette industry in the 1990s;

(2) there is significant price competition in some markets where interdependence is acute, such as the global video games market in the 1990s during the period 2001 to 2005 and thereafter.

The Sony-Microsoft game from 2000 to 2004 is discussed in the following pages of this chapter. The Bertrand challenge is explained by:

(1) realisation of the Nash equilibrium,
(2) Folk theorem benefit-cost condition,
(3) asymmetric sameness in price condition and
(4) error in the game.

Realisation of the Nash Equilibrium

We explore the first challenge in Figure 9.2. The point of intersection is the Nash equilibrium price for both players. It is neither an equal price nor a profit maximising price. It also does not represent an equilibrium where both players have equal market shares. It is the best outcome for each player given the reaction of the other player.

Figure 9.2 also shows the intersection of the reaction functions (R_A and R_B) of the companies. A price war will persist up to the intersection point of the two reaction functions. This is the Nash equilibrium price. For an example, refer to the Sony-Microsoft game dimension 2000–2004 in McNutt (2008).

Figure 9.2
Bertrand Modified Model

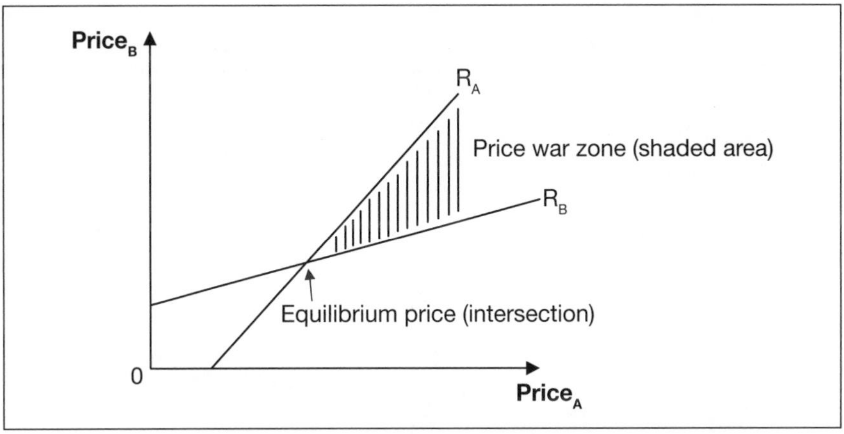

The process here is to observe the Nash equilibrium from the observed signals. It is at price band (149, 149.99) as illustrated later in Figure 9.4. This is the best price that both players could have achieved given the reaction of the other player. Management observe the signals ex-post and begin to reason strategically in a process called **backward induction** (see Chapter 7) by plotting the CTL and the reaction functions illustrated in Figures 9.3 and 9.4, respectively.

Figure 9.3
Critical Timeline — Sony *vs* Microsoft

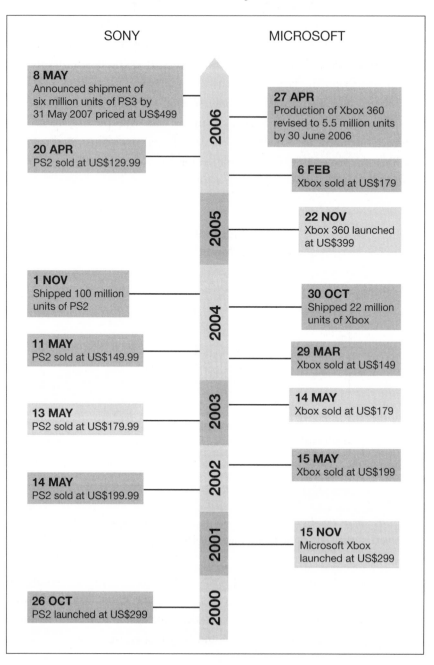

Figure 9.4
Nash Equilibrium — Sony *vs* Microsoft

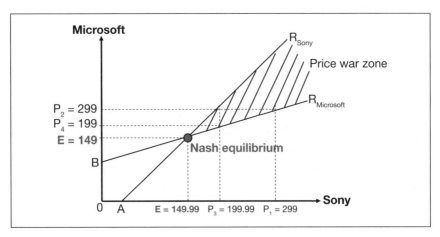

If the fact finder informs both players at price point 299, the history point, that:

(1) they were about to enter a price war and

(2) the best price for each would be in the range 149 to 149.99 after four years of price competition,

neither player would believe him. This is the classic PD, as both players believe that they can do better. It is important to note that the NE price is not the best in terms of maximum profit or maximum market share; it is simply the best in the game play given the reaction of the competitor.

Folk Theorem Benefit-Cost Condition

A second explanation is found in a formal agreement to fix prices above the Bertrand competitive level. Due to antitrust laws, it is illegal in most jurisdictions. The Folk theorem does not focus on formal collusion; rather, the term 'cooperative pricing' is used to refer to situations where firms can sustain prices in excess of those that would arise in non-cooperative single-shot games. Put another way, suppose two firms are unilaterally setting prices that are near the prices they would set if they had successfully colluded with each other. Are there conditions to do with costs and profits which neither firm would wish to undercut its rival? Under these conditions, cooperative pricing is feasible.

However, much remains unclear over the substitution of accounting on profit for economic profit, particularly if, as noted by Demsetz (1973), monopoly profits of the incumbent are capitalised in the accounting value of the firm's assets, notably patents and trademarks. In most cases, the only hard number is the market share and the concepts of dominance and significant market power are defined with respect to a market share threshold. Landes and Posner (1981) have argued that market power should not be defined in terms of specific market shares, but "to interpret the market share statistics in each case by reference to qualitative indicia of the market elasticity of demand and the supply elasticity of the fringe firms". They continued to argue that if the market elasticity of demand or the elasticity of supply were high, different inferences would be drawn from the defendant's market share than if either or both elasticity values were low.

Asymmetric Sameness in Price Condition

An asymmetric sameness in price is asymptotically close to a bargained competitive price. Therefore, it follows that not all instances of parallel behaviour give rise to the same strength of inference that parallelism results from anything other than the independent commercial judgement of firms. Parties that engage in tacit collusion behave quite differently from firms that enter into explicit cartels. Management of firms which engage in tacit collusion may not even know what they are doing; they may not recognise that the pricing practice supports an anti-competitive equilibrium. In many markets, price can take on a momentum of its own. For example, demand for a limited supply will increase price under the basic law of supply and demand. Conversely, in a competitive environment price will fall to a low level on its own momentum.

Consider two outcomes: incumbents have excess capacity that signals a threat to new entrants and a market with excess capacity that is not attractive to enter. A combination of both outcomes could result in a mixed duopoly where both firms simultaneously decide whether to enter the market and to communicate this decision. Eventually, they play a Cournot-Nash game by choosing output — rather than price — to compete against each other. Barro (1972) has shown that a mixed duopoly may lead to an improvement in allocative efficiency. For a fact finder trying to understand the proper context of the type of competition in a market, the actions and reactions of the firms should be regarded as an evolving process in which each participant performs its duty in the market as efficiently as possible. The basis of any 'understanding' is an increase in market power with a concomitant increase in allocative efficiency.

Competition or antitrust law and policy is about maximising consumer welfare, and it can only be achieved with lower competitive prices at the retail level. The perfectly competitive price that competition promises continues to elude the consumer across many product and service markets. If we begin with the premise that a market is a classic case of signalling — where the ability to 'do a deal' and negotiate or conduct transactions at prices through signalling mechanisms may be the *modus operandi* — the fact that a bargaining mechanism such as cartel arrangements or signals exist at all reflects the nature of the business. The fact that a bargaining mechanism cannot be easily monitored by others would make it difficult to detect instances of alleged price fixing.

Regret Matrix: Opportunity Cost

A price signal, Δp, from one player may not always lead to a matching price reduction. Furthermore, it does not require an immediate Δp if the player has a commitment to altruistic behaviour. When the first player observes that the second player is not following with a Δp, it may stop and reconsider the Δp. If so, the second player has influenced the first player not to initiate Δp, in effect changing the behaviour of the latter. Under these circumstances, the fact finder would observe cooperation and proceed to dismiss the possibility that it could have emerged from nothing more than the cold calculation of self-interest. It does not need to rely on a credible mechanism.

One important signal for DQ2 is the intention of DQ1 in reducing the price initially: Was the intention to start a price war unavoidable, using it as a catalyst for greater competition? DQ1 with CV = 0, for example, could be interpreted as a naïve strategy, especially when DQ2 reacts with a price reduction. Both DQs find themselves in a price war, but DQ2 would have to ask: Did DQ1 intend to initiate a price war? This is the error in the game — incomplete information can trigger off a price war. It also raises the issue of time constraint: Does DQ have a binding time constraint to complete the action?

With error, DQ1 may have a lower bound on price which facilitates intersecting reaction functions. Otherwise, DQ2 might believe that DQ1 is moving to the zero-price equilibrium. If DQ2 is going to follow with a price reduction (as perceived by DQ1, that is, CV ≠ 0), there is no reason why DQ1 should initiate a price war. Conversely, if DQ2 has CV ≠ 0, it will not initiate a price war. The price tumble that triggers off a price war scenario is more likely to manifest itself with asymmetric information, where one DQ is informed of all the parameters but a second DQ is not informed about a competitor DQ's aversion to a price war or willingness to engage in one.

It depends on how the DQ views pay-offs in the game. There is an element of regret in not taking an action. The costs of regret would have to factor in the costs of playing the game. This is discussed in McNutt (2008). In Table 9.4, assume you are player A with two strategies, S1 and S2. Player B has two strategies, S3 and S4. You only play S1 if the pay-off of 3 is the maximin. If you are player B and player A has played S1, you play S3 only if the pay-off of 4 is your minimax.

Table 9.4
Regret Matrix

	S1	S2
S3	3	4
S4	5	1

Maximin Strategy

In Framework T/3, we advocate that it is more rational for management to think in terms of the opportunity costs rather than the gains in a pay-off matrix. Consider a player faced with three options: S1, S2 and S3. The player has a CV. For illustration purposes, the pay-offs are defined in Table 9.5.

Faced with a decision, management that assumed the minimum pay-off may take a pessimistic view of the market-as-a-game. Therefore, they should act to ensure that they get as large a pay-off as possible in the market-as-a-game. This is called the **maximin** because it maximises the minimum pay-off. Thus, management are faced with two choices, S2 and S3, and are indifferent between them. This is sometimes called the criterion of pessimism, in that the worst is always assumed. Alternatively, management may be an optimist and choose the maximax strategy which maximises the maximum pay-off, leading to the selection of S1. Note that different criteria lead to different choices. If this were not true, then, as argued by Moore and Thomas (1976), "all criteria would lead to the same action suggesting that we might as well use a pin to pick out criterion" (page 44).

However, there is a third criterion that considers the opportunity cost of choosing a strategy. Referred to as the regret criterion, it is illustrated by pay-offs in a regret matrix. To better understand it, we convert the original pay-off from Table 9.5 into Table 9.6.

Table 9.5
Maximin

Action	CV = 0	CV ≠ 0	Minimum	Maximin	Maximum	Maximax
S1	10	1	1		10	10
S2	9	3	3	3	9	
S3	5	3	3	3	5	

Table 9.6
Regret Criterion

Action	CV = 0	CV ≠ 0	Maximum regret	Minimum of maximun regrets
S1	0	2	2	
S2	1	0	1	1
S3	5	0	5	

If, in retrospect, CV = 0 is correct, choosing S1 would be the correct choice and management would not incur opportunity loss or regret measured by the difference between the pay-off for the chosen strategy and that for the optimal strategy, S1, with CV = 0. If the game is unprofitable to player A, he should always use a maximin strategy. In other words, if player A cannot hope to obtain **more** than his maximin pay-off, he should adopt a strategy that will absolutely assure him of at least that much (Harsanyi, 1977).

In the mid-1990s, Motorola was emerging as a significant player in the mobile phone market — a nascent market that has grown exponentially over the past ten years. In many countries, there are more mobile subscriptions than people. In retrospect, Motorola had CV = 0 with respect to a small, obscure Canadian start-up called Research in Motion (RIM) which was targeting a new mobile email market. Had RIM not succeeded, Motorola would have had no regret in their choice of strategy that underestimated the mobile email market potential.

Saddle Point Market Shares

If the game under consideration is a zero-sum game that is strictly adversarial between players, maximin-minimax provides a unique stable equilibrium solution. In many markets, the market shares are consolidated in the sense that should one firm gain 2 per cent, it translates into a 2 per cent loss for one or more competitors in the market. The game is about market shares, and this is not an unreasonable assumption to make across many product markets for two-player games.

Consider two players, A and B, in Table 9.7. Assuming that player A has the strategy set (S1, S2 and S3) represented across the rows and player B can react with strategies (S4, S5, S6 and S7) represented in the columns, what should player A do when faced with the market share pay-offs? If player A is sure that player B would respond with S4, S1 is the optimal strategy for player 1 since it would get 95 per cent of the market share. Given player B's response of S4, strategy S1 yields the largest pay-off for player A and the worst pay-off for player B. Thus, player A can be certain that player B will not respond with S4 (Cole, 1973).

Player A must assume that player B will respond with S5, which gives the latter 95 per cent and leave it with only 5 per cent. By assuming the worst possible response, player A predicts that the outcome for his use of strategy S1 will be the minimum pay-off, that is, 5 per cent of the market. We illustrate this in **bold** print in Table 9.7. It would appear reasonable for player A to reject S1 as too risky. For player A, the strategy offers an almost all-or-nothing gamble. It depends on how player B responds. Therefore, player A chooses another strategy. S2 offers the possibility of 90 per cent if player

Table 9.7
Saddle Point Matrix

	S4	S5	S6	S7	Row minimum
S1	95	**5**	50	40	5
S2	60	70	**55**	90	55
S3	30	35	30	**10**	10
Column maximum	95	70	55	90	

B can be counted on to respond with S7. However, there is also the possibility that player B will respond with S6, thereby allowing player A a market share of 55 per cent. This is the smallest market share for player A if he uses S2. Again, we print it in **bold**.

If player A considers S3, the smallest market share is 10 per cent if player B responds with S7. Player A notes the least attractive outcome for each strategy. In a zero-sum game, player A assumes that player B will deploy a strategy that reduces player A's market share to a minimum. Thus, player A uses a **maximim** strategy, that is, the maximum of all the minima which is S2. Conversely, player B will select the highest possible outcomes in terms of player A's pay-offs that provide the column maxima of 95, 70, 55 and 90 illustrated in *italics*. Therefore, to obtain the highest market share, player B chooses a strategy that forces player A to the lowest of the greatest possible outcomes.

Accordingly, player B chooses S6 which allows player A a market share of 55 per cent. By confining player A to the least of the greatest shares, player B is said to be employing a **minimax** strategy, that is, choosing the minima of the column maxima. We conclude that the game does have a unique equilibrium. The market share of **55** per cent is both the maximum of the row minima and the minimum of the column maxima. If player A chooses S3, player B will respond with S6; if player B decides on S6, player A replies with S2. The market share of **55** per cent is referred to as the saddle point of the game.

Games are defined as *normal form* — illustrated by payoff matrices — or *extensive form*. In the extensive form, they allow management to transfer strategy choices onto a decision tree. Information which shows that player 2 is committed to avoiding a price war — but player 1 is not — can be transferred onto different branches of the decision tree, as illustrated in Appendix A1.3 (Nissan *versus* Toyota). Player 2 then faces the option of a counter-strike if a price war ensues. In this case, the non-cooperative solution is the dominant solution used to analyse games in normal or extensive form. The main property of the non-cooperative equilibrium is optimal response. If A knows B's action, at the non-cooperative equilibrium A will have no desire to change his strategy as he cannot improve. The same holds for B.

This gives rise to the Nash equilibrium, the best outcome a player can obtain given the moves or actions of other players.

Minimax: Is There Always an Equilibrium?

Consider two players, A and B, in the game of manufacturing cigarettes. If player A produces a king-sized (KS) cigarette and player B selects a filter, the former ends up with 20 market share; under zero-sum, the latter has 80 (see Table 9.8). Player A's best decision or strategy choice is not fully obvious. If it opts for KS, the reward could be 60 or 20 while the strategy of regular size yields 80 or 10. Management at player A might decide on a 50:50 probability of player B adopting either of its strategies. Thus, they evaluate the strategy of KS at 50 of 20 and 50 of 60 = 40. The alternative could be 50 of 10 plus 50 of 80 = 45. On the balance of probabilities, player A's best choice would be the regular-sized cigarette.

Let us examine this in greater detail. Player B is known to player A and both players are deemed rational. If player A produces a KS cigarette, player B would cut the latter's market share to 20; if player A selects regular length, it will secure only 10 market share. Hence, player A should pay attention to the worst outcome (minimum) of each strategy and be content with the **maximin** pay-off of *20* and chooses KS. Similarly, player B plays **minimax** as it considers the best that player A could do in response to each of its strategies and chooses the strategy that minimises the maximum pay-off to player A. Thus, if at best player B goes for filter, player A gets 20; if player B goes for unfiltered, player A gets 80. The minimax is *20* from the pair (20,80).

Table 9.8
A's Maximin = B's Minimax

	B (Filter)	B (Unfiltered)
A (King size)	*20*	60
A (Regular size)	10	80

If player B chooses filter, player A can do no better than to choose KS (regulars will give only 10). Player A's best response to player B's minimax filter strategy is its own **maximin** of KS, and player B's best countermove to player A's maximin is its minimax. However, do we always have an equilibrium outcome? Consider the market shares in Table 9.9 adapted from the original pay-offs in Baumol (1965).

Table 9.9
Loading the Dice

	B (Filter)	B (Unfiltered)
A (King size)	20	60
A (Regular size)	80	10

The **maximin** strategy for player A is still KS and the maximin pay-off is 20. However, player B's **minimax** strategy and pay-off is now unfiltered and 60, respectively. In this case, player A will choose to play KS, player B will choose unfiltered and player A will be surprised to receive 60. If player B opts in advance to believe that player A will adopt a **maximin** KS strategy, it will no longer think it wise to play the game with the unfiltered cigarettes strategy. Instead, it will switch to a non-minimax strategy and play a filter cigarette strategy. In this case, player A's pay-off remains at 20. Thus, we have mixed strategies with player A playing maximin and player B playing a non-minimax strategy; it is to player A's disadvantage (not securing an elusive 60) to have its plans guessed by player B. Therefore, player A could respond by 'loading the dice' and play a mixed strategy. For player B, the key question is: What will player A do, and how will player A reshape its strategy?

Trust: The Core of the Bertrand Dilemma

Do you trust your partner? Should you trust your competitor? Ultimately, trust depends on one's belief about other people, be they competitors or otherwise, in the business world. If A trusts B to do X, the latter — knowing that A trusts him to do X — has a choice to make: Does he do X, or not? The consequences of X are of interest in the business world. One scenario, referred to as the **moon-shot**, is the belief that X will occur. Neither A nor B issued the moon-shot, neither knows that about the other and they behave as if the moon-shot has happened. Another scenario is the extent to which trust is credible in terms of doing X, where X has significant negative consequences for both A and B. In this cartel scenario, both players must trust each other completely.

Combat competition refers to entry at the margin and manifests itself when an increase in the number of firms do not pose an advantage for the market system. Contest competition differs from it in that the market is unequally partitioned — some firms are content with their market share while others are the targets of mergers or takeovers. A contest would occur, for example, when individual firms compete either for market share or market position. Contest competition can be seen as a mechanism that maintains the market level of concentration as long as the number of firms do not change. One essential characteristic of contest and scramble competitions is that there is no exit of firms below a threshold level of concentration as there is ample market share for all competing firms.

Above a critical threshold level of concentration, exit increases abruptly in a perfect scramble. However, it is a gradual development in a perfect contest. This follows from the requirement that contest leaves a constant number of firms in the market system. We contend that almost all competition under normal market conditions falls between the two extremes of contest and scramble. This may be a key contributor which undermines an understanding of antitrust analysis that competition and concentration are antithetical. In antitrust folklore, concentration leads to collusion; if we accept that competition and concentration are not antithetical, the debate in antitrust will turn on concentration. Collective dominance would become uncomfortable — and possibly untenable — if it leads to the conclusion that competition contributes to collusion in a market system. However, it may be possible — at least in theory — to enunciate the possibility of competition with monopoly outcomes. Pure contest is rare; as individual firms compete for market share, a compromise is often reached as combat competition becomes more intense and average market share may be reduced.

Stigler's Dilemma

Players avoid price wars. They are expensive. One option is to form a cartel. Stigler (1964) argued that firms seek cartelisation. The gains from cartelisation include a less elastic demand curve and a slower rate of entry. It is rational and may be commercially sound for modern firms to collude. Therefore, no amount of legislation will stifle that desire. In US antitrust, parallel pricing falls under Section 1 of the Sherman Act, where the courts focus attention on the type of evidence "from which a conspiracy can be inferred". In this instance, the type of behaviour referred to is conscious parallel behaviour. However, as we know, the difficulty in antitrust lies in deciding whether parallel behaviour is sufficient to establish an agreement. A not dissimilar debate took place in EU competition circles over the court's interpretation of collective or joint collusion in the Gencor/Lonhro case (McNutt, 2005). The argument can be traced to Sraffa (1925) who argued that firms would avoid competition if the expected rents from cartelisation exceeded the gains from long-run competition. This forces us to focus on the type of competition in a market and not on market structure *per se*: scramble, combat and contest. Alternatively, if management enter a signalling game, the risk of competition could be avoided.

Across the literature, it is clear there is a need to return to an understanding of the type of competition that prevails in a market that is under scrutiny, with a focus on firms interacting in an evolving Boolean network of interrelated firm behaviour. As the atomistic behaviour of a perfectly competitive market structure leads to a long-run equilibrium, likewise the Boolean behaviour of the market systems evolves into an ordered arrangement that manifests itself as market-sharing strategies and, inevitably, implicit or parallel collusion on price. In a market system, the firm is an integrated network of signalling and decision making. As argued elsewhere, greater emphasis should be placed on the relevant firm rather than on the relevant market in antitrust analysis.

   With different elasticities, for example, a two-firm and a ten-firm market structure challenge the traditional economic theory underpinning antitrust policy. A ten-firm structure with an industry elasticity of 0.5 could be more monopolistic — measured on the Lerner Index — than a two-firm structure with an industry elasticity greater than 1.5. In the Chamberlin model, the degree of industry elasticity determines the level of profit. Can we imagine an industry structure that exhibits an oligopoly structure with zero long-run profit? The problem is that the industry structure is defined in the traditional structure-conduct-performance model with reference to the concentration ratio of market shares (H) and market demand elasticity (η), thereby deriving the equation

$$L = \frac{H}{\eta}$$

   However, this equation does not depend on any form of explicit collusive behaviour. Rather, the monopoly power arises from the exogenous assumption of Cournot-Nash play and the restriction on entry. These conditions assure an outcome which, according to Cubbin (1988), could be interpreted as an 'apparently collusive arrangement'. Ironically, the monopoly equilibrium arises from the best-reply responses in what is essentially a non-cooperative Cournot-Nash competition.

Trigger Price

An equally important determinant is the DQ's knowledge of the elasticity of its suite of products. At its simplest, elasticity measures the responsiveness of any quantity, Δq, to changes in price, Δp. The concept can be expanded to include supply-side responses and quantity-type variables on the demand side. The most interesting concept is the advertising elasticity of demand which measures, for example, how a percentage change in advertising expenditure would contribute to changes in sales. Earlier in the book, this has been referred to as price elasticity (of demand). For a linear demand, the elastic region lies above the mid-point and the inelastic region below the mid-point. The real market price is found in either region. Hence, strategically speaking, DQ should interpret a price fall as the movement towards the mid-point and a price increase as the movement upward towards the mid-point. How do we distinguish between the two? We do so by computing that mid-point, the trigger price, and identifying the likely responsiveness in the direction of the price signal.

In the elastic region, as price falls, sales increase and revenue goes up; conversely, revenue falls if price rises. Therefore, price and revenue are inversely related. On the contrary, in the inelastic region, price and revenue are positively related. Now, a management decision to change price must assume knowledge of such a price — the trigger price. If price is to drop, it can do so only from the elastic range towards the mid-point. Otherwise, management fail the total revenue test. Such failure is a strategic mistake if the price change excites a price war by sending the wrong signal to rival players. If anything, the need to compute the trigger price acts as a guide. It is not a real price that can be charged to consumers; rather, it is a measure of the amount by which a price **ought** to change in any price sequencing.

What Market to Enter?

Chandler's hypothesis is that the structure of a market — defined by the number of firms — follows the strategy adopted by the firms in the market. The boxed feature on the following page introduces the critical strategy questions that firms need to ask themselves. In Framework T/3, there is a game embedded strategy (GEM*s*) which has the following additional characteristics. First, the determination of the preferred market depends on a host of factors discussed throughout the book, from sustaining a competitive advantage to strategic positioning in the market and playing the non-cooperative game of competition. Secondly, management's best response depends on the unique set of circumstances they face, although management may differ by type and the threats facing the firm or how the firm should respond.

Game Embedded Strategies (GEMs)

Strategy Question: What Market Should We Be In?

A company should NOT be in a market where the identity of the nearest competitor is not known, OR where the identity is known but not the likely reactions.

Dimensions of GEMs

1. Profits are captured by management as players. Porter's Five Forces strategy focuses on the threat to industry profits, Framework T/3 identifies new opportunities for growth and GEMs enable management to act to capture and retain profits in t+1.

2. GEMs are more likely to be ahead of the game in terms of the next strategy adopted in oligopoly markets. They facilitate a second mover advantage and — with no surprises — a first mover advantage is obtained.

3. Participation in a game requires management to pay attention to signals, camouflage their type and be both consistent and coherent over the life of the game.

Strategic Focus

Dell Inc represents an interesting case (see Figure 9.5). Competing on non-price attributes is a new approach for Dell and propels it into new strategic territories.

All players would like to differentiate themselves significantly so as to remove their nearest rival from the horizon. In Dell's current strategic position, this could mean moving to the non-price competitive Cournot box with $CV = 0$. However, Dell has a historic type — a Baumol type — of using price to drive earnings, revenues and value, and whether it keeps to type can be gleaned from signals in its CEO's statements and fiscal performance.

Figure 9.5
Dell's Movement in Strategic Focus

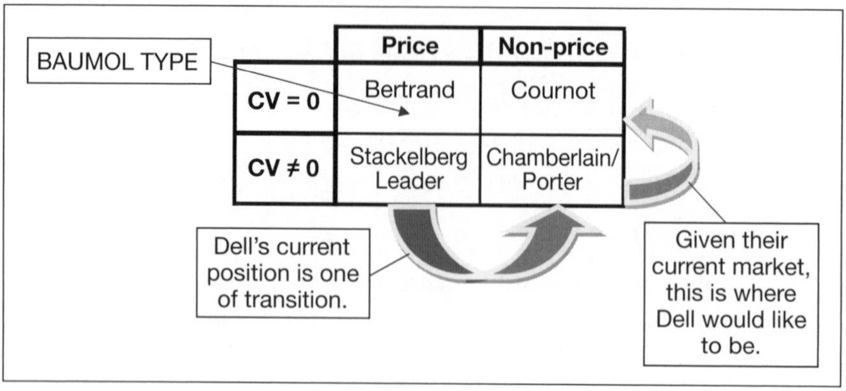

BAUMOL TYPE	Price	Non-price
CV = 0	Bertrand	Cournot
CV ≠ 0	Stackelberg Leader	Chamberlain/ Porter

Dell's current position is one of transition.

Given their current market, this is where Dell would like to be.

Drawing on Framework T/3, game theory can be used to play out scenarios to determine which strategic options are optimal. This is important for taking the leap from strategic option to strategic decision. The toolbox presented in this monograph can apply to business strategy at different levels — corporate, divisional or regional. All of them have one starting point: the goals of the organisation. When goals are known and understood, management seek to implement strategies to achieve them. Tactics determine how each strategy is played out on a daily basis. The toolbox incorporates game theory. There are many analysis tools and models for deriving business strategies, including Porter's Five Forces model and the Value Net. They can be deployed to support management as players in a dynamic, non-cooperative evolutionary game.

The toolbox is a process that starts by requiring DQs to understand organisational goals. It then moves on to demand an understanding of the industry in which the company operates and the factors affecting the industry and its future. Through this analysis, opportunities and challenges are identified and result in strategic options that may benefit from being played out as a game — the next stage in the process. Game scenarios help to determine the optimal strategic option. Furthermore, game theory lends insight into the factors that are important in undertaking the chosen strategy, such as where to compete, price sensitivity of the market and how firms structure themselves to compete effectively. The process ends with a strategic decision, which is the outcome of strategic game playing.

Business strategy can be interpreted as games of complete information where management not only know their own type, but also the type of competitors. Incomplete information is introduced by vertical blending, whereby the type of management blends with the type of player and the preferences of management are clouded. In this context, by adapting the arguments of Harsanyi (1977), we are able to assume that each player has a particular characteristic which determines its preferences on actions (social states) and its beliefs about the Z-preferences of other players, the competitors. A key characteristic is whether the player is an incumbent or an entrant. The nomenclature on type depicted in Figure 9.6 should help clear the air.

Figure 9.6
Nomenclature on Type

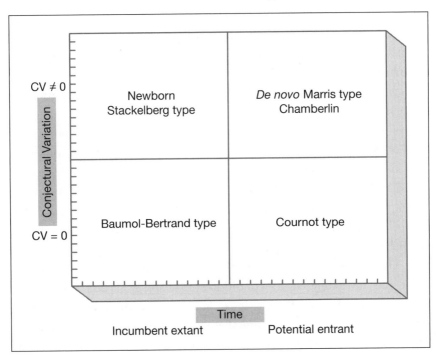

In other words, with vertical blending the type of player is no longer common knowledge in the game. To have assumed that the beliefs of players are common knowledge in the real world of business strategy appears unreasonable. In reality, we have little idea how individual management actually acquires beliefs. However, vertical blending allows us to define the players in a game by their strategies. Therefore, we do not ask: How do management behave? Rather, we ask: Given their strategy, how should they behave? The focus is on answering: What market should they be in? There is less focus on answering: How can they optimise in the present market? Management make a decision that something must be done to improve financial performance, and then take an action on how and when to improve that performance. The action depends on their understanding of type and the realisation that their company is a player in a market-as-a-game.

GEMs Strategy Toolbox

Of all the pay-off matrices, self-interest (maximising the size of the pay-off) governs the likely response of a player. The fact that the probability of the outcome is not relevant can be diluted through the introduction of the behavioural characteristics of players. In assessing the game dimension, management should pay particular attention to understanding the behavioural characteristics of players in the game — as well as their type — and assessing the likely responses of players based on a set of assumptions, beliefs and prior knowledge. The key point to note is that game pay-offs can be adjusted to reflect the nature of the response by players, given the assumptions made about their behaviour. Management should derive a set of behavioural aspects about other players in order to factor in the likelihood that the behaviour will affect game pay-offs.

The majority of pay-offs in the game analogies referred to in this book can be extended to conditional probability. From a review of the concepts of game theory, it is clear that the discipline can add a different perspective and complementary approach to the examination of strategic business decisions. Many of the key elements in game theory provide insights into areas such as competitor reactions, pricing, cooperation and competition, the importance of scale, the value of information, signalling and the importance of communication. The concepts of adverse selection and signalling provide valuable direction and insight on how to compete. Game theory broadens the scope of economic analysis.

In their collaborative work, Duncan Easterbrook and the author have constructed a strategic toolbox to incorporate game theory (see Figure 9.7). Game theory can be used to play out scenarios to

Figure 9.7
Easterbrook–McNutt Strategic Toolbox GEMs

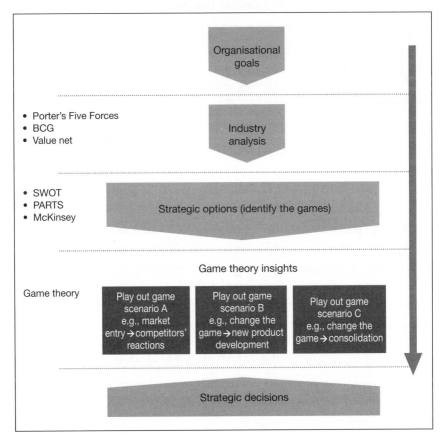

determine which strategic options are optimal. This is important for taking the leap from strategic option to strategic decision.

Faustian Belief

It is critical to understand the future implications of one's action in time period t. One is reminded of Goethe, who tells us that Faust lost the liberty of his soul when he said to the passing moment, "Stay, thou art so fair".

In Table 9.10, the win-win Faustian payoff (2,2) for both players is to play SA and signal type.

Table 9.10
Prisoners' Dilemma

	SA	SB
SA (Signal your type)	2,2	–1,3
SB (Act differently)	3,–1	0,0

Samuelson (2005) reported that in laboratory experiments on PD games, some players preferred the more superior outcome (2,2). In the business context, where the market is a game and type is either signalled by all players or analysed by third parties, the DQ player may prefer the more equal outcome (2,2) of SA to the more asymmetric outcome (–1,3) under SB. If both players adopt SA, we observe a **penguin strategy** — a credible, collective response by competitors to a market event such that no one competitor acts unilaterally and all competitors are observed to behave together. It can give rise to an accidental sameness in price (ASP) — that is, an adherence to the same price may not necessarily be sufficient evidence of tacit collusion — as argued by McNutt (2005). It may well be that competitors do compete in a market system of observed cooperation. A defining characteristic of GEMs is knowing when to cooperate and when to compete.

Boolean Competition

> Not one of them was capable of lying,
> There was not one which knew that it was dying
> Or could have a rhythm or a rhyme,
> Assumed responsibility for time.
> —**W.H. Auden**

I n the market-as-a-game, competition is a process and the game is necessary because of its function in determining evolving market systems. The process could be described as efficient contracting between firms. In an evolving market system, competition can be viewed as an assignment of property rights to the market system rents or profits (McNutt, 2005). Management should enquire whether the (p,q) pair is a strategic outcome, and whether it is stable in an evolving market system. In other words, will (p,q) persist? If a firm chooses their actions from that pair, will the choice of price and quantity continue to distribute profits to the firm? In an evolving game, the ability to choose may well turn out to be a disadvantage (Maynard Smith, 1982). Apple Inc is a classic example — it could launch a low-priced smartphone or iPhone 6 or a new innovation in 2013. If a player believes that its action may not deliver a first mover advantage in the game, it may decide not to move. This is tantamount to there being no choice for the firm as a player in the game.

Market Systems

A market system is an evolving game in which competition is described in terms of its net effect on the players in the game. Decoding strategy provides a conceptual framework, T/3, for the discussion of competition in the market-as-a-game. It also assumes that there is a **Boolean network** of behaviour across the competing firms — the players in the game. The Boolean network provides for a decision which stipulates that each firm in a market with n firms acts (say, on price, R&D expenditure or innovation) if, and only if, two or more firms act. For example, firm A makes a decision if two other firms do so as well, but each firm can decide whether to act at each decision point.

While this can be generalised to explain the quintessence of aggressive competition, its central message is that for a random firm in an evolving market system its behaviour on price and quantity may be fixed exogenously. For example, a random firm offers n products and for each feasible bundle q, it charges a price p(q). Profit is strictly a function of the prices. Each customer responds by choosing its preferred bundle and paying the price. The firm's objective in choosing the price is to maximise its profit, obtained as the difference between the revenues collected and the costs incurred to supply the bundles. The firm incurs this cost only if a customer purchases a non-negative amount of some product. The prices evolve as marginal prices (Wilson, 1991), since they are observed as partial sums of the associated prices for incremental bundles of product.

Network Effects

The standard economic model of collusion begins with the assumption that it does not cost a thing to form and maintain cartels. However, cartels do accrue costs, such as monitoring cheats. Johnsen (1991), in a classic article on assignment of property rights to cartel rents, argued that "maximising cartel wealth translates into maximising the discounted value of the difference between gross cartel rents and cartel enforcement costs" (page 189). The closer the cartel comes to the (p,q) that maximises gross cartel rents, the greater the incentive for members to cheat.

The key to applying the concept of tacit collusion is to distinguish it from competitive aggressive behaviour. In any defence of an alleged price-fixing case, the mere fact of adherence to prices may not establish an agreement to follow them (McNutt, 2003). Therefore, it would be unlikely for a court to find that adherence alone could prove — beyond all reasonable doubt — an agreement to adhere to prices; there may be 'an asymptote in prices' (ASP) observed as an accidental sameness in price across the market.

In Figure 10.1, market shares are denoted by S. The introduction of a zero-sum assumption implies that as the market share of firm 1 (S_1) increases, that of firm 2 (S_2) decreases. This is noted in the left-hand quadrant and represents a classic case of real competition characterised by aggressive competitive behaviour through loss in market share. The history of market price is represented by $P_i(S_i)$, which is asymptotic to a lower bound, $P = LMC$, the long-run competitive price of the market in which these two firms interact. The loss in market shares that accrues to any one firm is represented by Δ_w.

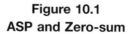

Figure 10.1
ASP and Zero-sum

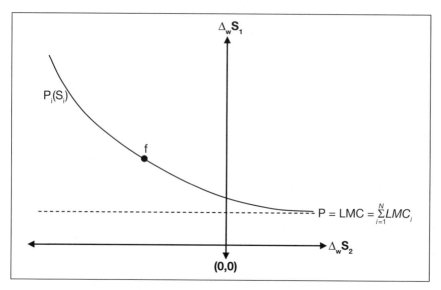

The Boolean network provides a competitive zero-sum rule, $\Delta_w x_i$, as follows:

$$\Delta_w x_i = x_i - w_i = \{(1, -1), i = 1 \text{ and } (-1, 1), i = 2\}$$

Markets can be either collusive or competitive. However, in both situations firms behave rationally and independently. Tacit collusion needs some form of enforcement mechanism to sustain a coordinated equilibrium at f in Figure 10.1. Without a credible mechanism, the market price at f could be described as moving towards a long-run competitive price. It is the market characteristics and history of prices that make a market more collusive and less competitive. An ASP price standard is asymptotically close to a long-run competitive price. Therefore, it follows that not all instances of parallel behaviour could give rise to the same strength of inference that parallelism results from anything other than the independent commercial judgement of the firms in a Boolean network.

Price Coordination

Economic theory would have us believe that price coordination is designed to reduce the uncertainty associated with interdependence and to decrease the likelihood of mutually destructive price competition. Consider n-player rent and profit games. The player set — the set of firms $\{1, 2, 3, \ldots n\}$ — is denoted by N and the set of coalitions by 2^N. Such a game is a real valued function v: $2^N ->R$ with v(0), which assigns to each coalition, S, its worth v(S). The worth v(S) can be interpreted as the reward which the players in S can obtain by working together. We denote the set of n-person rent and profit games by G_n. For analysts, the main problem in cooperative game theory is how to divide v(N) amongst the players when a grand coalition is formed.

There are many solutions, and they offer economists and lawyers a new tool of analysis and set of defences, respectively. In some games, for example, the dividend of any player is proportional to the marginal contributions of each player to the grand coalition (Owen, 1982). Marginal contributions are captured by movements along the $P_i(S_i)$ function in Figure 10.1. This is analogous to the biological concept of 'carrying capacity', that is, the maximum number of firms that can be sustained by a given amount of resources. It is not unlike an optimal club size in the provision of public goods (McNutt, 2002). Later in this chapter, we include it as the parameter K in the equations for contest competition. Intuitively, one knows that not every firm can adapt to external threats; with the passage of time, only a few large firms survive.

Perfect information would allow some businesses to quickly enter the price-fixed markets and compete away the supra-competitive profits. The competition would soon drive prices down to only an insignificant fraction above the competitive level (Averitt and Lande, 1997). As the industrial (business) stage in different jurisdictions assumes the status of an oligopoly, there may be increasing support for the argument that a measure of price coordination is necessary in an oligopolistic industry. Innovation may compel firms to enter into complex contracts and relationships with other firms to bring technology to the economic market. However, the level of uncertainty is especially high for the development and commercialisation of new technology. Accordingly, innovating firms may need to achieve greater coordination than what the price system can bring about on its own (Jorde and Teece, 1990).

Scramble, Combat and Contest

Imagine n operating firms in a market that is viable for only m < n. For example, this may be the case in markets where technology or innovation involves a fixed cost of production. Selection may occur so that firms do not lose money. Fudenberg and Tirole (1986) have examined how the remaining firms were picked to explain why selection was not immediate, that is, the existence of time periods over which firms lose money but do not leave the market. They find it difficult to pin down a stable equilibrium outcome and conclude that there is a strictly positive — but possibly small — probability that the firm, as a player in a game, 'enjoys fighting'.

Put another way, a firm with strictly positive duopoly profit never drops out of a market — staying in the market is a dominant strategy. Biologists have also analysed this type of situation. For example, animals may spend time or energy in a seemingly useless fight for prey (Maynard Smith, 1974). Firms may persist in a market. If firm 1 observes that firm 2 is still in the market at time t, it ought to infer that firm 2 has a positive duopoly profit and will not drop out. Thus, firm 1 ought to leave if it has a negative duopoly profit.

Moore's 'Form of Friction'

The fluctuation in the population of firms describes the process of competition. In the early history of economics, the economic principles of Marshall were the subject of debate by Sraffa (1925) and Hotelling (1929) who laid the intellectual foundations for the concept of imperfection in the market. Moore (1906) also offered a critical observation which has influenced the discussion in this chapter: "What is the nature of the limitation of the applicability of propositions under the hypothesis of perfect competition? The almost invariable answer to this question is that the imperfection of competition is simply *a form of friction*, producing for the most part, a negligible variation from the standards that prevail in a regime of perfect competition" (page 211, italics added).

At the turn of the 20th century, the rigours of biology and physics were available to aspiring economists intent on developing an intellectual foundation for economics. Writing in the 1890s, Alfred Marshall had opted for the rigours of physics rather than the mathematical modelling of ecological systems when drafting his path-breaking *Principles of Economics*. May (1973) commented that such models aim to provide a conceptual framework in the discussion of broad classes of phenomena. The question raised by Moore could only be answered in the context of an understanding of the evolution of firms and markets. In trying to understand what Moore meant by 'friction', we introduce types of competition based on models of inter-species competition in biology (Hassell, 1976).

Economics is about human behaviour. Since the 1990s, new research has led to the development of behavioural economics and evolutionary game theory. This research has evolved from the seminal work of Kahneman, Maynard Smith, Price, Strotz, Thaler and Tversky over many years. The interested reader can consult the excellent article by Pesendorfer (2006) for a full citation and review of the research.

Observational learning has been discussed by biologists for many years. From a reading of the research described by Page (1999) on animal intelligence, for example, one can argue that the behaviour observed in the animal kingdom — how animals compete and co-operate with each other as well as how their behaviour evolves over time — offers a serious benchmark in our attempt to reach a fundamental hypothesis on how players in a game behave as humans in a social or business setting.

Types of Competition

One type of competition is **scramble competition**, where there is equal share of the market and equal effects of competition between the competitors. Scramble may be manifested by changes in the size or number of firms. A second type of competition is **combat competition**, where the acquisition of market share requires constant defence. This is characteristic of a more stable market system. Combat competition may involve entry at the margin and manifests itself when an increase in the number of firms is not advantageous for the market system. Finally, in **contest competition** the market is unequally partitioned, whereby some firms are content with their market shares while others are the targets of merger or takeover bids.

Under normal market conditions, it is conceivable that competition falls between the two extremes of contest and scramble. Pure contest is rare; as individual firms compete for market share, there is often a compromise as combat competition becomes more intense and average market share may be reduced. Larger firms will evolve and survive as they provide economies of scale in production and innovation. Thus, large firm size is essential to the success of innovative activity. With economies of scale, large firms can have sufficient resources to undertake innovative activity.

This process is not dissimilar to Schumpeter's (1934) cycle of 'creative destruction' whereby old industrial structures, products, manufacturing processes and organisational form are continually changed by innovative activity. Schumpeter theorised that economic growth occurs through a process of 'creative destruction' and long-term growth is intricately linked with innovation. The introduction of a new good or quality, new method of technology, new organisational form or new market are all characteristics of a market system.

Before we can understand how a market system differs from a market structure, we need to acknowledge that firms cannot easily adapt to an external threat. The classic monopoly firm has little or no incentive to change if the status quo is profitable. Incumbents may attempt to retard entry. The classic monopoly and the incumbent both suffer from a 'box-ticking exercise' whereby behaviour and conduct are predetermined by the market structure. It is as if the very structure of the market creates what Nolan and Croson (1995) called 'structural inertia'. In contrast, firms evolve in a market system and make radical changes in both strategy and organisation in response to external threats. For example, the s-firm is an internal response from the workers and management to the external threat of unemployment.

Modelling Contest Competition

Contest would occur, for example, when individual firms compete for a given market share or market position. Contest competition can be seen as a mechanism that maintains the market level of concentration as long as the number of firms do not change. An essential characteristic of contest and scramble is that there is no exit of firms below a threshold level of concentration as there is ample market share for all competing firms. Above this threshold level, exit increases abruptly in perfect scramble but gradually in perfect contest. This follows from the requirement that contest leaves a constant number of firms in the market system.

There is entry and exit of firms in the market system. The specification of the entry function and its concavity in Chapter 6 highlighted the restrictive nature of entry. E(q) translates into actual market share if entry is impeded. In a market system, all firms (potential entrants and incumbents) have the potential to grow exponentially, as expressed by the system equation

$$\frac{dn}{dt} = r.n$$

Thus, the rate of change in the number of firms, n, with the passage of time, t, is the product of the numbers of firms and their intrinsic rate of natural increase, r. This is the maximum instantaneous rate of increase under the conditions for competition outlined by Scherer and Ross (1990). To find the number of firms at time t, we integrate to derive

$$n_t = n_0 \, e^{rt}$$

where n_0 is the number of firms at time t_0. From this, we can plot the exponential growth in the number of firms over time. However, no firm can sustain such an increase for long. Competition for resources will become increasingly more acute and the net rate of increase $(\frac{dn}{dt})$ will be reduced, either through mergers or acquisitions, exit of firms or both.

Therefore, the market system can be described as

$$\frac{dn}{dt} = r.n \left\{ \frac{(\beta - n)}{\beta} \right\}$$

where β is the 'carrying capacity' of the system at a point in time — the maximum number of firms that can be sustained with limited resources. If we use the firms' production levels at $t \geq 0$ as a proxy for the amount of limited resources, the carrying capacity could be defined as

$$CC = \frac{(\text{Firm's production levels})^{-n}}{\{n/n + 1\}^n}$$

The emphasis is on the available carrying capacity at $t \geq 0$. Knowledge of rising scale of economies may not be available to the fact finder at $t = t_0$. The number of firms may fall as they merge to enjoy efficiencies. The available carrying capacity plays an important role in determining whether a merger may lead to a dominant position or market share may converge on a collusive outcome. Using integration, we have

$$n_t = \frac{\beta}{\{1 + q.e^{-rt}\}}$$

where $q = \frac{\beta}{2}$ is the point of inflexion on the time axis as illustrated in Figure 10.2 (adapted from Varley [1973]). The growth in the number of firms can be described as sigmoid. It commences almost exponentially, but as the number of firms increase there is more and more feedback from the term $\{\frac{(\beta - n)}{\beta}\}$ which represents the effects of increased competition. In contest competition, a rapidly growing firm may be more likely to make a horizontal acquisition because it is better able to use the additional capacity. The net rate of increase declines until there is no further change in the number of firms when the carrying capacity is reached, $\{n_t = \beta\}$. Therefore, the market system is in equilibrium, $\{n^* = \beta\}$.

The model offers a stable equilibrium since the number of firms will always return to the equilibrium level following an external threat

Figure 10.2
Scramble (Path A) and Contest (Path B)

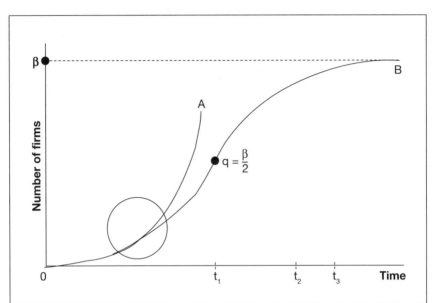

or disturbance. For example, a declining firm operating under diseconomies of scale is more likely to sell and exit the system. Tremblay (1987)
found that a firm with large economies of scale will have a greater
incentive to merge if these are multi-plant in nature. The economic
phenomenon observed at $t \geq 0$ is contest competition; the maximum
number of firms is independent of the initial density of firms.

Spherical Competitors

The basic condition of the market system, the carrying capacity, can
plausibly explain its evolution. The litmus test is whether the fact finder
can define the market in an evolutionary system. Much depends on what
the fact finder observes at the critical juncture in the evolution of the
system, as illustrated by the circle in Figure 10.2. The point of departure
in the circle can be changed by the internal dynamics of each firm in
the system. Path A is the exponential evolutionary path, which may not

be sustainable — it represents intense, aggressive competition with both entry and exit of firms. It may, for example, characterise atomistic perfect competition in classical economics. However, when surviving firms have established a level of market share, path B can better describe the logistic evolution of a system that is more closely aligned with the evolution of markets in classical economics: from a starting position in a competitive market to the emergence of monopoly firms and an oligopoly structure capped at β.

In concentrated markets where five or fewer players enjoy 100 per cent market share, the zero-sum constraint allows each player to infer what the other player is likely to lose by his action. Without knowing the market share of a player, for example, a rival does not know whether an action on price will be meaningful. If the action is described as a price dwarf and a rival reacts at time period t, knowledge of market share is invaluable as without it a reaction to such a price action could trigger off a price war.

Technology has a long history that dates back many centuries. From the ox cart to the car and the mainframe to the laptop, techno-logy gaps are diminishing and consumer expectations are increasing. Many players are moving under the influence of each other's tech-nology pull. Some are moving unexpectedly fast as though pulled by an invisible, time-dependent set of preferences. The β is defining the process of competition. The players are spherical competitors since technology allows competition from every angle. Observations of the signals — together with managerial theories about how management behave and evolve — all point to Framework T/3. In a market system, the number of players, n, is reduced in time ($\mp$,t). Thus, the process of competition, β, can be captured by the equation

$$\beta = n \, \frac{d\mp}{dt}$$

The author is working on a draft paper that combines Metcalfe's Law with the $\{n^* = \beta\}$ equilibrium.

Figure 10.3 captures a stylised game pay-off between players A and B on price commitment. The pay-offs are computed by Yang-

Figure 10.3
Hsu–McNutt Signalling

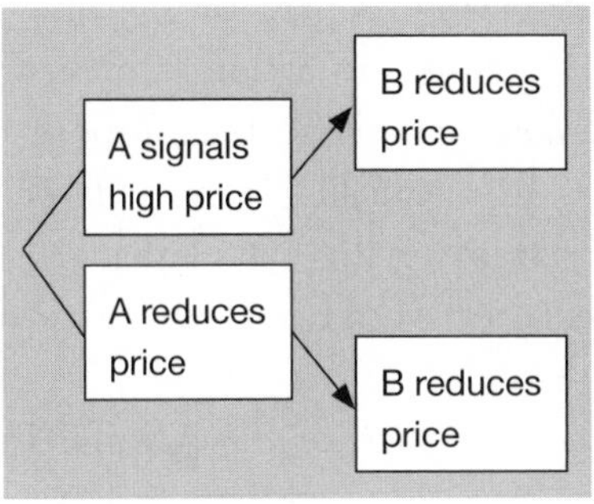

		B Signals high price	B Reduces price
A signals high price	B reduces price		
A reduces price	B reduces price		
A Signals high price		(4,3)	(3,4)
A Reduces price		(5,1)	(1,1)

Chan Hsu and the author (McNutt, 2010a) to illustrate existing Nash equilibria in terms of the best one can do given the reaction of a competitor and the elusive (4,3) that could be secured with price leadership — provided both players trust each other not to deviate from the agreed price leadership. The game dimension — in terms of the near-rival — may differ according to geography. For example, Nissan and Toyota are near-rivals in Japan, but in Europe the players could be Nissan and Volkswagen. Notwithstanding geography and type, an equilibrium requires a degree of trust and commitment.

Critical Reflective Thinking *versus* Updating

In this book, we argue that type is a function of signals; a signal is the first derivative of type with respect to time. At time $t = T$, individual players learn from each other through signalling. When a player's signal is observed by management, a type is revealed. At that moment, management must reflect on the signal critically and must not be under the illusion that a game of action and reaction is likely to begin. When management has filtered the information from the signal, a game of action and reaction is observed.

In the case of a moon-shot (see Chapter 1) from player A, player B believes that the signal will translate into an action by player A. Player B proceeds to act and is observed by other players (including player A) in the game who learn its actions by observing its play. By signalling a moon-shot, player A stops and begins to think; no action is observed at t = T. This is referred to as a *do-nothing strategy*, the purpose of which is to force another player to act. In a signalling game, player A exercises power over player B's belief system to the extent that it can get player B to do something that the latter would not otherwise do (Lukes, 1974).

In a Bayesian game, probabilities are assigned to the payoffs. The player depicted in Chapter 1 as Leo the Liar — whose type is ascribed 'liar' — may choose to act honestly. If he does, at least one other player will have incomplete information on Leo's type. As players, management in the market-as-a-game can be described as participating in a Bayesian game and the signals on type are critical to the playing of the game. It is generally agreed amongst game theorists that in a dynamic (also known as extensive) Bayesian game of incomplete information, players discover their opponents' types by observing their play. This is because each move by a player reveals new information on its type. With no new information, there is a challenge for a Bayesian market-as-a-game if others do not know, for example, that player A in Figure 10.3 has betrayed his type — deceiving other players by signalling a high price but reducing the price during the game. When player A evaluates or updates his belief about player B without reference to the formation or *origin of the belief systems* of either player, he is engaged in Bayesian updating. Why would Leo the Liar betray his type and act honestly? A Baumol type may not react in a price game. Therefore, competitors should ask: Why would a rival player be observed as doing nothing in a game?

In a normal form Bayesian game of incomplete information where payoffs are represented in matrices, the players are unable to update their prior beliefs on opponents' types. One way to model incomplete information is to reduce uncertainty in the game by constructing a CTL and convert it into a game of imperfect information on patterns. In this case, player A knows only his own type; other players who do not know his type observe his signals.

Neo-Rational Action

To learn from others in the market-as-a-game, players must understand what we refer to as the Humean neo-rational action of a player (McNutt, 2010b) — that is, a player betrays his type during a game by signalling X but do Y. If management want to do Y (reduce price) and believe that doing X (signal a high price) is causally necessary to do Y, reason dictates that they signal X in the game. If player A plays Y and lowers the price — this action is confirmed by observation (of a lower price) by others of the action of playing Y — it is a neo-rational action: he may obtain a pay-off of 5. In other words, player A has fooled others into thinking that he is thinking about playing X prior to his decision to do so. He has created noise in the game by signalling X and doing Y — possibly to obtain a pay-off of 5 or he may do nothing.

The market-as-a-game may be a dynamic game in the sense that information about the economic characteristics and type of other individuals in the game is incomplete. Regardless of whether player A believes player B, it is the convergence of their interdependent actions that leads to an equilibrium. The neo-rational equilibrium could occur at pay-off (4,3) for both players in Figure 10.3 if player A is secure and player B thinks that the latter is thinking about playing X, both players signal a high price and the high price is obtained in the game.

Blind Squirrels Find Nuts

Bayesian equilibrium only takes into account the fact that players may learn their opponents' actions by observing their play. The Bayesian approach ignores a neo-rational action and it does not suggest a model on the origin of prior beliefs. In Framework T/3, beliefs are updated in the absence of new information. This arises because management must focus on the origin of their belief about a competitor's likely action. As players in the market-as-a-game, management observe their opponents' types by observing their play; if no play or action is observed, management learns by signalling. Hence, individual players are acting rationally at $t = T$ when they do not ignore their own information about signals but ignore the actions of others.

In Framework T/3, a signal can influence the action of a player in a game. For example, in Figure 10.3, if at t = K < T player B signals a Baumol type by signalling sales revenue targets, this strongly implies that its prices will fall. However, observing lower prices in a game at t = T does not necessarily mean that player B is a Baumol type. For example, if a new technology or functionality was added to its product at t = K — creating an inelastic demand for the product — player B will increase price to maximise total revenues. Therefore, if the probability of lower prices in the absence of a Baumol type is greater than zero, the probability of lower prices with a Baumol type is less than one since the probabilities sum to one.

On the other hand, if lower prices did not happen when player B was not a Baumol type, the observation that prices are lower at t = T in a game with player B would always confirm that it is a Baumol type. Strategic reasoning is not the product of a very high probability that Y leads to X, or that a lowering of price signals a Baumol type. It is, however, the understanding that a very **low** probability that **not-Y** ($\sim$Y) could have led to X. An error occurs in the game when too much attention is paid to $p(X|Y)$ and not enough to $p(X|\sim Y)$ in determining how much evidence X is for Y. The degree to which a result X is evidence for Y depends not only on the strength of the statement "we would expect to observe signal X if Y were true", but also on the strength of the statement "we would not expect to observe signal X if Y were not true". If player B in Figure 10.3 is a Baumol type and always reduces price, it is rational for him to signal type and obtain the pay-off 4 in (3,4) provided player A does not lower price. With that knowledge, player A — as a secure player (Chapter 7) — signals a high price, trusting B to do likewise. For player B, a 3 in pay-off (4,3) is preferred to a pay-off of 1 in (1,1).

Strategy is about player action and reaction. In an interdependent, non-cooperative game, it is a rule telling management which action to choose at any given time. Game embedded strategy is about knowing when and how to act. Interdependence is recognised, beliefs are formed and management rethink the strategy of 'going it alone' in order to obtain a competitive advantage in the market. Heraclitus, a Greek philosopher of the sixth century BC, wrote, "Character is destiny";

Framework T/3 recognises that management type is destiny, and that an understanding of type — coupled with an understanding of technology and time — is intricately linked to sustaining a competitive advantage in the market-as-a-game.

For management, the key objective is to obtain a competitive advantage in the market. However, sustaining that competitive advantage against spherical competitors is a daunting challenge facing management today. In any game, it is critical to decode the strategic moves of an opponent; in the market-as-a-game, it behoves management and strategists alike to decode strategy in order to sustain a competitive advantage. Their opponents are doing it!

Yellow Snowflakes

In every game, everyone learns through evolution — evidence of an inherited *hardwiring* according to Page (1999). However, individuals in competitive and non-cooperative games find themselves compelled to learn by using information. Framework T/3 focuses on information on player type and presents a simple play: defection, dishonesty and cheating are dominant strategies while cooperation yields a higher pay-off. Bernard Mandeville's 18th-century paradox in the *Fable of the Bees* — that of 'the venerable feud in human nature between the forces of self-interest and the forces of altruism' — is embedded in a Prisoners' Dilemma-type game, where it is rational to betray and cheat in the game.

However, if a player's behaviour appears related to that of their competitors' in games in which they win rather than in those which they do not, it suggests something that is observable by the players but not by an observer. Recently, Zitzewitz (2012) commented that a "collusive scheme is one, and arguably the leading, candidate for such an observable". Each player displays a pattern and the series of action-reaction moves creates a sequence of unobserved random events which — upon close examination — reveal a strategic pattern.

Embedded in this strategic pattern are moves. These moves are not only interdependent in the sense that the individual player abandons unilateral action, but they betray what appears to be a connected pattern of moves. Intuitively, companies — as players in the market-as-a-game — are enveloped by the process of remembering patterns rather than facts. What is observed is either an accidental sameness in price (McNutt, 2005) or the presence of *phoretic* competitors hitching on the success of other players in a game. These competitors assign an equal probability to all available pairs of (p,q) and select one at random. They will reduce the price one day and follow it up with a new product launch on the next.

The strategic issue here is not whether a player reduces the price today, but rather how the price reduction today fits into the observed pattern. Therefore, before a judgement can be made on the rationality of the move, a third-party observer should examine his or her own preferences and implicit beliefs *in loco parentis* — how the player *feels*. In terms of new developments on the concept of bounded rationality in the literature on neuro-economic theory, Brocas and Carrillo (2008), for example, have argued that our limited ability to process information leads to judgement biases.

To understand the biases, one may build different behavioural theories based on casual evidence models such as the CTLs and pattern analyses provided in the Appendix. In this book, we have argued that players are enveloped by the game. This arises due to the mismatch in signals, the trustworthiness of other players, the speed of reaction, the frequency of moves and imperfect information on player type; collectively, these factors impact on a player's sequence of moves.

There are many instances in which the players do adjust their beliefs. For example, I may have misread the signal or you may be lying. We refer to this as a **yellow snowflake** as it takes time to know another's type: I learn from your actions, but your type changes and so I ask, 'Do I really know your type?' Google may ask: Will Apple Inc launch a low-priced nano iPhone in 2013? Likewise, Apple Inc may ask itself: Should we launch a nano iPhone before the signalled launch of Google's new Moto X smartphone in October 2013?

Snowflakes do not come in yellow — or do they? They are uncommon at a point in time. In 2003, there was no iPhone — and no Google smartphone. Knowledge of past actions may help to reduce the uncertainty of future actions. In the sequence of random events, the occurrence or non-occurrence of an event at time period t depends not only on the sequence *per se*, but also on the frequency of the events, the *Griselda effect* of keeping to type, the speed of reaction and the creation of sub-games. When is it time for the gambler to leave the gambling table? The timing may be a function of his previous winnings, so he may choose to leave when he is broke. However, his timing may be a function of the frequency of the events, speed of reaction and creation of sub-games.

If Leo the Liar is unwilling to enter the truth camp, for example, this helps to inform us on Leo the player. A yellow snowflake descends on the game: either Leo keeps to type or other players believe that he will keep to type. The guilt that Leo feels from opting out of the truth camp is likely to be dependent not only on others' belief about his trustworthiness, but also on the nature of the relationship between him and his opponent. If the opponent assigns a high probability that Leo will join the truth camp — despite the fact that Leo will not join — the opponent's belief would be considered irrational because it conflicts with the evidence.

Nevertheless, nothing prevents the opponent or any player — enveloped by the game — from holding such beliefs. Apple Inc and Google may truly be influencing each other's belief systems. Their respective management teams have now entered the *true state* of 'I think–You think–I think'. In other words, they are decoding strategy as each thinks the opponent would think, feels as the opponent would feel and gains insights into how beliefs are determined. A yellow snowflake has descended upon the game.

Critical Timelines
of Real-World
Companies

The following pages offer a selection of critical timelines (CTLs) that represent different companies as players across different markets-as-a-game. Each CTL identifies the game dimension in terms of the **geography** of the game and the **process**. The process includes product, technology or innovation as defined in the book — consumers do not buy products, but functionalities or characteristics. In the case of Starbucks, the process is the 'coffee experience'; for Geely, it is the technology acquired from Volvo. It could simply be the product, as in a can of Pepsi, but a broader definition facilitates a richer dataset of signals.

Each CTL was constructed during case preparation in the MBA Workshops and the team affiliations for each case are credited in the Acknowledgements. The cases are a representative sample of analysis and include Apple, Geely, HSBC, Microsoft, Nissan, Nokia, Pepsi and Starbucks. In each case, the game dimension G is defined with respect to geography and process and a time period of five years. The objective is to identify a pattern in the signals and to identify the near-rival — that competitor in the sum of competitors who is more likely to react first.

A game, G, occurs when player A acts and player B reacts. A sub-game, g, occurs when a sequence of moves appear reversed as player A reacts to player B. The sub-game can be observed in the CTLs of Microsoft and Pepsi. The decision tree in the Nissan case allows us to define an extensive form of the game as observed. The HSBC case includes causality in the share price performance. Further examples of the casual link between CTLs and key performance indicators can be found on **www.patrickmcnutt.com** in the icon 'eLearning and Games Academy'.

The pattern observed provides an insight into the player's strategy set, that is, the sequence of moves in the market-as-a-game. If it is only a pattern of price signals, a Bertrand pattern has been observed; if it does not include price signals, a Cournot pattern is observed. The research can be intense; over three days of gathering market intelligence, each group assembles the collected intelligence into a CTL and presents a hypothesis.

Noisy Edge of Strategy

Each hypothesis is debated and defended. Information about the company — extracted from company accounts, analysts' reports and media sources and portals — is researched in great detail and analysed before it is filtered into a sequence of random events. The sequence is called a critical timeline (also referred to as CTL). The events are defined as signals. In order to ascribe a pattern to the signals observed, a control factor is required — the *Nash premise*. The premise states that an action is followed by a reaction from a near-rival who is likely to react first amongst the competitors.

The sequence of moves in a CTL enables an observer to see the pattern at a moment in time — from a *glimpse* (no pattern) to a *snatch* (a pattern) to a *momentary insight* (an explanation of what is observed). Patterns always exist, repetition will occur and prediction is inevitable over time. CTLs evolve and mature over time, culminating in the Nash equilibrium. The distance — measured in days, weeks and months — between moves becomes shorter as competitors react faster to each other's move in the game. What the moves have in common with each other is an embedded predictability. The CTLs presented in this book represent the noisy edge of business strategy.

Working on the premise that the act of observing a pattern alters what is being observed, the research groups were cautioned to observe the signals and construct a pattern — but not to judge. The pedagogy to ask is: Do you know more about the company after the CTL is completed than when you first did before you started? If the answer is yes, the CTL morphs into the habitat of strategic actions. It behoved the research groups to know this habitat even as they observed the signals. Finally, they explored repetition in the pattern observed to determine what will happen in time period $t+1$.

Objective Reality

The case studies describe patterns and conclude that there is no such thing as an objective reality about a company's strategy. What we term 'objective reality' is really a consensus of business minds who think alike. For example, company A is a monopolist and prices are high; company B acts and company C follows. Thus, the patterns can be interpreted as footnotes to Kant who first demonstrated that we can never know the *noumenon* — the thing itself — but only the phenomenon, that is, the thing as it presents itself to our minds. We can never really know the pattern, but the patterns observed can help predict what is likely to happen next — the so-called *effects' effect*. Hypothetically speaking, the repetition of a pattern could accommodate both timing and causation of reactions to your initial action in a market-as-a-game.

If there is a pattern, can we find it? Once we find it, can we identify any repetition in the pattern in order to determine — with a degree of probability — what is likely to happen next? Information about an individual can be found in one's pattern — type or signature, methods and timing; collectively, one's game credentials. One is now a player in a game. If one keeps to type, there is the *Griselda effect*. Honesty occurs when there are credible signals of honest behaviour — player B is honest and nice (McNutt, 2009). Because players are dishonest or lying, learning arises with positive probability.

From the earliest work of Huizinga (1955) to Schelling (1960), Price (1970) and the modern research of Kahneman (2011), it is widely accepted that human (and animal) behaviour can be explained by learned behaviour. In T/3, as players management are enveloped by the game with an innate drive to observe others who are in similar circumstances — as measured by performance indicators on share price or market share. They evaluate their respective outcomes and take feelings away from the game. Like a sponge in water, each player absorbs the game. They adapt to the game, invest in their type and signalling skills and transform their strategy. Observed behaviour which is transcribed as a pattern into the CTL should be regarded as a window into the mind of the decision-maker. Management enter the *true state* of 'I think–You think–I think' and think as the opponent would think, feel as the opponent would feel and gain insights into how beliefs are determined.

By providing an action-reaction stochastic game framework for pattern assessment, Framework T/3 brings together three attributes that have always been present; collectively, they frame an action observed at a point in time. A Baumol type player, for example, signals a price decrease. Each opponent can decide whether to play the game. If the decision is to play, do one play with a perfect signal or without any information on type? By recognising that there are many variables that one does not observe, the CTL in effect randomises the information on corporate intelligence. It is frustrating, but it is the frustration with corporate intelligence and the construction of a pattern that brings order to random events. Viewed as a pattern, the random unobservable variables and events can be balanced with information on type and signals. The researcher is not accepting or rejecting a hypothesis, but is observing a pattern.

In the literature on games, arguments have been made that unreliable information is more expensive than reliable information, and that strategy evolves in a game to become more flexible as a game embedded strategy. As defined in the book, in the context of individual behaviour observational learning is influenced by the observation of other players' actions not only *because of the information contained therein* (Bandura, 1977), but also because of the information on type. The act of observing translates what is being observed into a strategic pattern. This pattern is a valuable piece of information. The strategist or fact finder either observes the strategic pattern or fails to do so. It is neither a case of cause and effect, nor is it about being right or wrong; it is about the insight gleaned when one observes a pattern arising from a chain of action-reaction events at a point in time. Thinking about other players' actions is the essence of decoding strategy.

Construction of Critical Timelines

The purpose of a CTL is to illustrate a sequence of events and to discover the pattern embedded in that sequence. Each player in the game will have a type — a signature type that defines its actions and reactions — and the speed at which the action-reaction sequence occurs. This provides a glimpse into the end game in the neighbourhood of the Nash equilibrium. The sequence of moves contains information on the play — frequency of the moves, timing of actions and reactions, emergence of sub-games and pattern recognition (either price moves or non-price moves).

Stage One: The Game Dimension

The game dimension, G, is defined by the geography of the game and the process. The process includes product, service, technology and innovation *inter alia* that delivers an end result to the consumer. The geography can be narrow (for example, Hong Kong) or broad (for example, Asia including Hong Kong).

The process can be as varied as 'the coffee experience' in a Starbucks game, number of stores by Tesco, product launches by Apple Inc (iPhone 2 to iPhone3 to iPhone 5) and Sony (PS2 to PS4) or R&D and innovation by pharmaceutical firms such as Pfizer and Ranbaxy. If the signals embedded in the pattern are price signals, we define the game dimension as Bertrand. Conversely, if the signals are non-price, we define the game as a Cournot game.

Stage Two: The Corporate Intelligence

The required information can be gleaned from sources such as company accounts, investment portals, analysts' commentary, expert opinion, data warehouses, Bloomberg, cnbc, Thomson Reuters and *Financial Times*. Video intelligence allows the researcher to read the signals from interviews conducted with key decision-makers in the company or by analysts.

Stage Three: The Sum of Competitors

The game dimension outlined in Stage One will host a number of competitors, but the one competitor of interest is the one who reacts first in a sequence of events. The researcher will define *what-if* scenarios to identify a family of CTLs in order to discover who will emerge as a likely candidate for near-rival from amongst the sum of competitors. Empirically, this can be supported by more sophisticated data analysis and pattern recognition, as well as by computing the cross-price elasticity in a Bertrand price game and conducting entropy analysis in a Cournot non-price signalling game.

Stage Four: The Conjectural Variation Filter

In addition, a filter can be used based on the belief system of the key decision-makers (the DQs) in the company as a player in the game. This enables the researcher to begin the construction of a CTL by filtering down to that competitor — the near-rival — who is more likely to react first given the game dimension. Once the filtering process is complete, pattern recognition occurs. Supported by strategic lateral thinking, the construction of *what-if* and *if-then* hypotheses allows the researcher to decode strategy.

Player A is considering a series of actions and the likely reactions from the sum of competitors B, C and D. Player A has a belief system: if it executes Action 1, it believes that only player B is likely to react; for Action 2, it believes that players B and C will react; and for Action 3, it believes that only player D will react. Through a process of elimination, player A is able to use the conjectural variation (CV) matrix as a filter to identify player B as a near-rival — that competitor in the sum of competitors who is more likely to react first across a series of actions in a game (Table A1.1).

Table A1.1
Player A's Conjectural Variation (CV) Matrix

	Player B	Player C	Player D	Near-Rival
Action 1: Lower price	$CV \neq 0$	$CV = 0$	$CV = 0$	B
Action 2: Launch new product	$CV \neq 0$	$CV \neq 0$	$CV = 0$	B or C
Action 3: New innovation	$CV = 0$	$CV = 0$	$CV \neq 0$	D

In a *what-if* scenario, a player creates a CV matrix to filter out those competitors who are likely to react to each action. If player A wishes to avoid player B in a game, it chooses Action 3. If, however, player A wishes to engage player B in an exclusive two-person game (a *Drusian* game of two-player action and reaction), a combination of Actions 1 and 2 should be chosen to engage the near-rival — player B. Only one player survives in a Drusian exchange, named here after Drusus Minor, an enthusiast of gladiator fights in ancient Rome.

Figure A1.1
Apple *vs* RIM

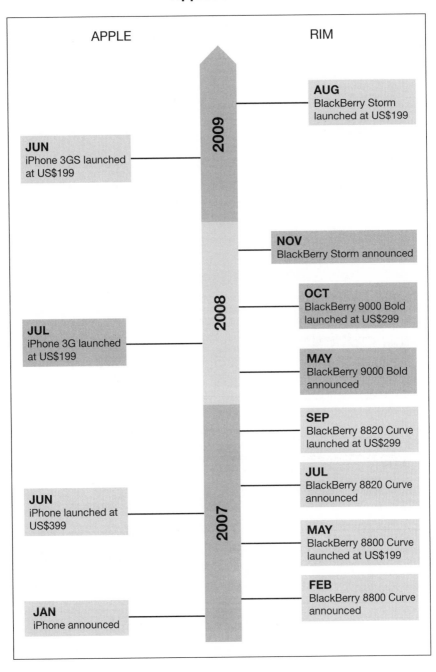

Figure A1.2
Geely *vs* Tata — Global Critical Timeline

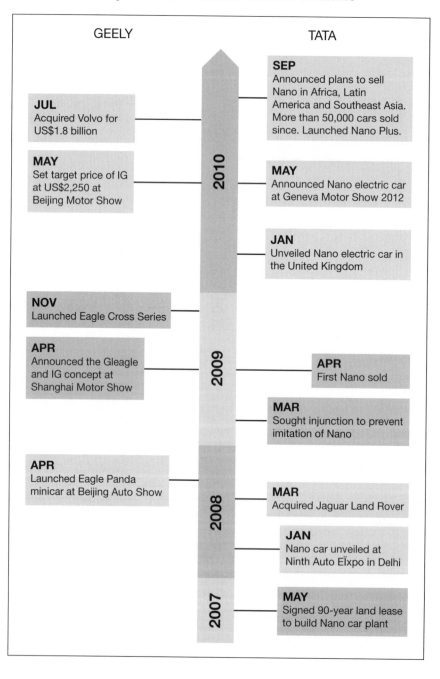

GEELY   TATA

SEP
Announced plans to sell Nano in Africa, Latin America and Southeast Asia. More than 50,000 cars sold since. Launched Nano Plus.

JUL
Acquired Volvo for US$1.8 billion

MAY
Set target price of IG at US$2,250 at Beijing Motor Show

MAY
Announced Nano electric car at Geneva Motor Show 2012

2010

JAN
Unveiled Nano electric car in the United Kingdom

NOV
Launched Eagle Cross Series

APR
Announced the Gleagle and IG concept at Shanghai Motor Show

APR
First Nano sold

2009

MAR
Sought injunction to prevent imitation of Nano

APR
Launched Eagle Panda minicar at Beijing Auto Show

MAR
Acquired Jaguar Land Rover

2008

JAN
Nano car unveiled at Ninth Auto EÏxpo in Delhi

2007

MAY
Signed 90-year land lease to build Nano car plant

Figure A1.3
Nissan *vs* Toyota (Decision tree)

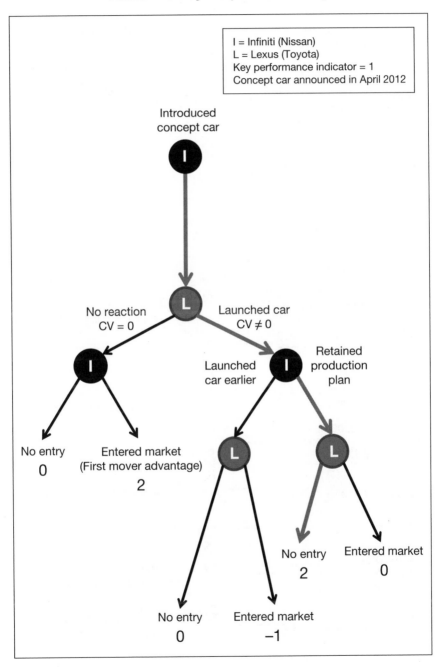

Figure A1.4
Nokia *vs* Samsung in China

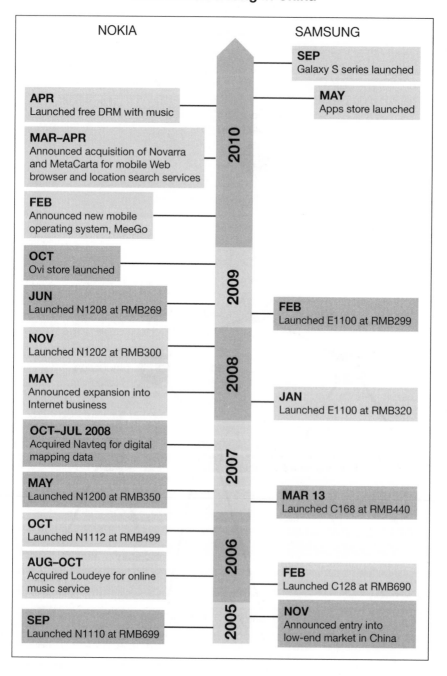

NOKIA

SAMSUNG

SEP
Galaxy S series launched

APR
Launched free DRM with music

MAY
Apps store launched

MAR–APR
Announced acquisition of Novarra
and MetaCarta for mobile Web
browser and location search services

2010

FEB
Announced new mobile
operating system, MeeGo

OCT
Ovi store launched

2009

JUN
Launched N1208 at RMB269

FEB
Launched E1100 at RMB299

NOV
Launched N1202 at RMB300

2008

MAY
Announced expansion into
Internet business

JAN
Launched E1100 at RMB320

OCT–JUL 2008
Acquired Navteq for digital
mapping data

2007

MAY
Launched N1200 at RMB350

MAR 13
Launched C168 at RMB440

OCT
Launched N1112 at RMB499

2006

AUG–OCT
Acquired Loudeye for online
music service

FEB
Launched C128 at RMB690

SEP
Launched N1110 at RMB699

2005

NOV
Announced entry into
low-end market in China

Figure A1.5
HSBC vs RBS (Time lag between key events for near-rivals in the game)

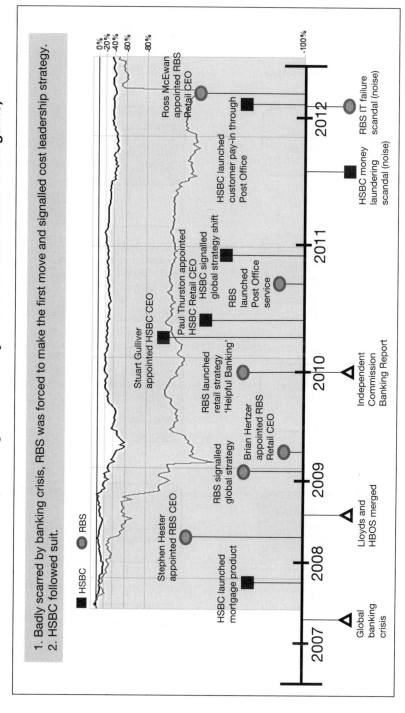

1. Badly scarred by banking crisis, RBS was forced to make the first move and signalled cost leadership strategy.
2. HSBC followed suit.

Figure A1.6
Microsoft *vs* Google

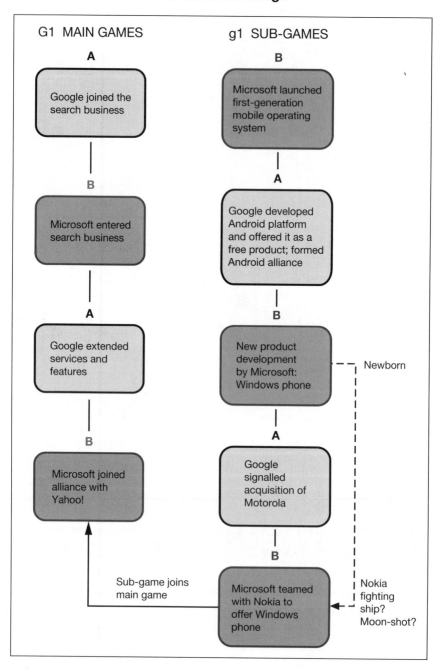

Figure A1.7
Pepsi *vs* Wahaha (Game G1)

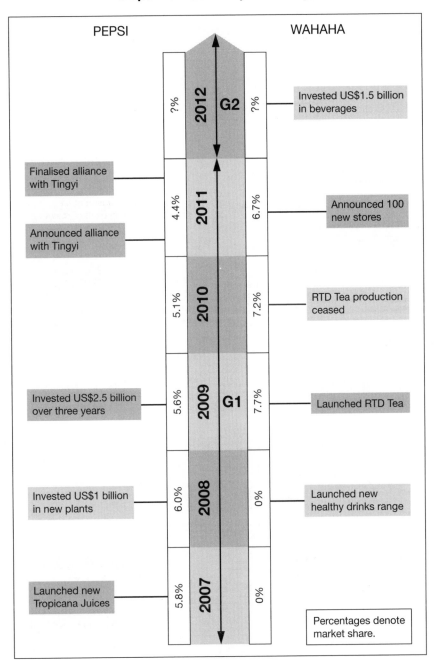

Figure A1.8
Pepsi *vs* Coca-Cola (Sub-game g1)

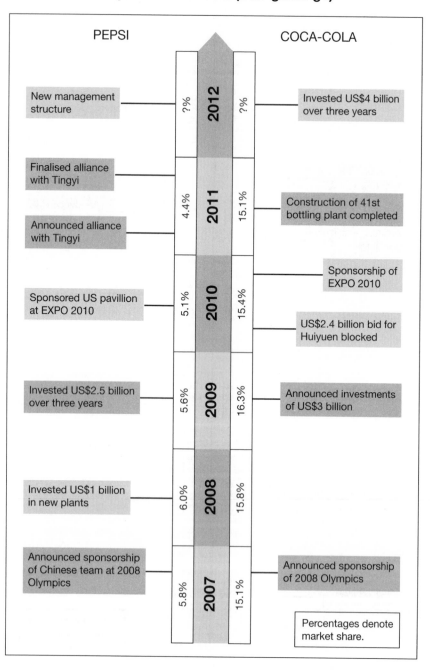

Figure A1.9
Starbucks *vs* Nestlé

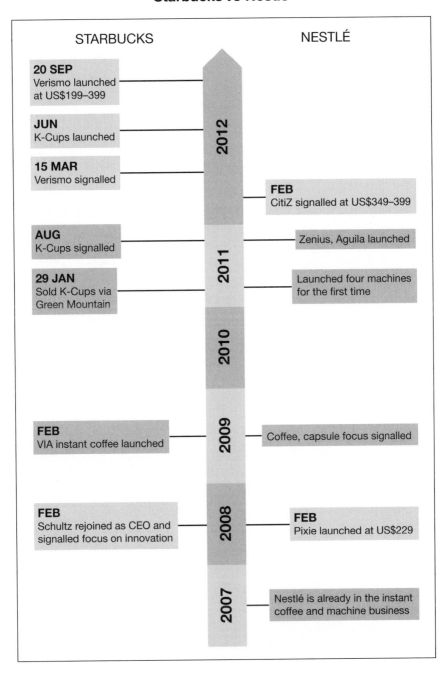

Bibliography

Averitt, N. and R. Lande. (1997). Consumer sovereignty: a unified theory of antitrust and consumer protection law. *Antitrust Law Journal*, Vol. 65, pp. 713–756.

Bandura, A. (1977). *Social Learning Theory*. Englewood Cliffs, NJ: Prentice Hall.

Barro, R. (1972). A theory of monopolistic price adjustment. *Review of Economic Studies*, Vol. 39, pp. 17–26.

Bartley, J. and C. Boardman. (1986). The replacement-cost-adjusted valuation ratio as discriminator among takeover targets. *Journal of Economics and Business*, Vol. 2, pp. 41–55.

Baumol, W.J. (1959). *Business Behaviour, Value and Growth*. New York: Macmillan & Co.

Baumol, W.J. (1965). Models of economic competition. In: P. Langhoff (ed), *Models, Measurement and Marketing*. Englewood Cliffs, NJ: Prentice Hall.

Baumol, W.J. (1967). Calculation of optimal product and retailer characteristics. *Journal of Political Economy*, Vol. 25, pp. 187–198.

Baye, M. (2008). *Managerial Economics and Business Strategy*. New York: McGraw-Hill.

Berle, A.A. and G. Means. (1932). *The Modern Corporation and Private Property*. New York: Macmillan & Co.

Besanko, D., D. Dranove, M. Shanley and S. Schaefer. (2013). *Economics of Strategy*, sixth edition. Hoboken, NJ: John Wiley & Sons.

Binmore, K. and P. Dasgupta. (1986). *The Economics of Bargaining*. Oxford: Basil Blackwell.

Brickley, J., C. Smith and J. Zimmerman. (2007). *Managerial Economics and Organisational Architecture*. New York: McGraw-Hill.

Brocas, I. and J. Carrillo. (2008). Theories of the mind. *American Economic Review*, Vol. 98, pp. 175–180.

Chamberlin, E.H. (1962). *The Theory of Monopolistic Competition*. Cambridge, MA: Harvard University Press.

Chandler, A.D. Jr. (1962). *Strategy and Structure: Chapters in the History of the American Industrial Enterprise*. Cambridge, MA: MIT Press.

Cole, C.L. (1973). *Microeconomics: A Contemporary Approach*. New York: Harcourt Brace Jovanovich, Inc.

Cox, B and J. Forshaw. (2011). *The Quantum Universe*. London: Penguin Books.

Crawford, V.P. and N. Iriberri. (2007). Fatal attraction: salience, naïveté and sophistication in experimental hide-and-seek games. *American Economic Review*, Vol. 97, pp. 1731–1750.

Cross, J.P. (1989). *Jungle Warfare: Experience and Encounters*. London: Arms & Armour Press.

Cubbin, J.S. (1988). *Market Structure and Performance*. New York: Harwood Academic Publishers.

Cyert, R.M. and J.G. March. (1963). *A Behavioural Theory of the Firm*. Englewood Cliffs, NJ: Prentice Hall.

Davies, H. and P-L Lam. (2001). *Managerial Economics*, third edition. London: Prentice Hall.

Demsetz, H. (1973). Industry structure, market rivalry and public policy. *Journal of Law and Economics*, Vol. 16, pp. 1–10.

Dennett, D. (1996). *Kinds of Minds*. New York: Basic Books.

Edgeworth, F.Y. (1881). *Mathematical Psychics: An Essay on the Application of Mathematics to the Moral Sciences*. London: C. Kegan Paul.

Ellsberg, D. (1961). Risk, ambiguity, and the savage axioms. *Quarterly Journal of Economics*, Vol. 75, pp. 643–669.

Follett, M.P. (1924). *Creative Experience*. New York: Longman Green.

Friedman, J. (2000). A guided tour of the folk theorem. In: G. Norman and J.F. Thisse (eds.), *Market Structure and Competition Policy: Game Theoretic Approaches*. Cambridge, UK: Cambridge University Press.

Friedman, J., P. Jehiel and J.F. Thisse. (1995). Collusion and antitrust detection. *Japanese Economic Review*, Vol. 46, pp. 226–246.

Fudenberg, D. and J. Tirole. (1986). *Dynamic Models of Oligopoly*. New York: Harwood Academic Publishers.

Gul, F. and W. Pesendorfer. (2007). Welfare without happiness. *American Economic Review*, Vol. 97, pp. 471–476.

Gurven, M. (2004). Does market exposure affect economic game behavior? The ultimatum game and the public goods game among the Tsimane of

Bolivia. In: J. Henrich, R. Boyd, S. Bowles, C. Camerer, E. Fehr and H. Gintis (eds.), *Foundations of Human Sociality: Economic Experiments and Ethnographic Evidence from Fifteen Small-Scale Societies*. Oxford, UK: Oxford University Press.

Hagstrom, R.G. (2005). *The Warren Buffett Way*. Hoboken, NJ: John Wiley & Sons.

Harsanyi, J.C. (1977). *Rational Behaviour and Bargaining Equilibrium in Games and Social Situations*. Cambridge, UK: Cambridge University Press.

Hassell, M.P. (1976). *The Dynamics of Competition and Predation*. London: Edward Arnold Publishers.

Hay, D.A. and D.J. Morris. (1991). *Industrial Economics and Organisation: Theory and Evidence*. Oxford, UK: Oxford University Press.

Henrich, J. (2004). Cultural group selection. *Journal of Economic Behaviour and Organisation*, Vol. 53, pp. 3–35.

Hofstadter, D.R. (2007). *I Am A Strange Loop*. New York: Basic Books.

Hotelling, H. (1929). Stability in competition. *Economic Journal*, Vol. 39, pp. 41–57.

Huizinga, J. (1955). *Home Ludens: A Study of the Play Element in Culture*. Boston: Beacon Press.

Imai, M. (1986). *Kaizen: The Key to Japan's Competitive Success*. New York: McGraw-Hill.

Johnsen, D.B. (1991). Property rights to cartel rents. *Journal of Law and Economics*, Vol. 34, pp. 177–203.

Jones, T. (2004). *Business Economics and Managerial Decision Making*. Hoboken, NJ: John Wiley & Sons.

Jorde, T. and D. Teece. (1990). Innovation and cooperation. *Journal of Economic Perspectives*, Vol. 4, pp. 75–96.

Kahneman, D. (2011). *Thinking Fast and Slow*. New York: Farrar, Straus and Giroux Publishers.

Koutsoyiannis, A. (1980). *Modern Microeconomics*. London: Macmillan Press Ltd.

Landes, W. and R. Posner (1981). Market power and antitrust cases. *Harvard Law Review*, Vol. 94, pp. 937–996.

Leibenstein, H. (1976). *Beyond Economic Man*. Cambridge, MA: Harvard University Press.

Lukes, S. (1974). *Power: A Radical View*. London: Macmillan Press Ltd.

Mahoney, J.T. (2005). *Economic Foundations of Strategy*. Thousand Oaks, CA: Sage Publications.

Mandeville, B. (1981). *Fable of the Bees*. New York: Arno Press.

March, J.G. and H.A. Simon. (1958). *Organizations*. New York: John Wiley & Sons.

Marris, R. (1964). *The Economic Theory of Managerial Capitalism*. London: Macmillan Press Ltd.

Marschak, J. and R. Radner. (1972). *Economic Theory of Teams*. New Haven: Yale University Press.

May, R.M. (1973). *Stability and Complexity in Model Ecosystems*. Princeton, NJ: Princeton University Press.

Maynard Smith, J. (1974). The theory of games and the evolution of animal conflict. *Journal of Theoretical Biology*, Vol. 47, pp. 209–221.

Maynard Smith, J. (1982). *Evolution and the Theory of Games*. Cambridge, UK: Cambridge University Press.

McCullough, M.E. (2008). *Beyond Revenge: The Evolution of the Forgiveness Instinct*. San Franciso, CA: Jossey-Bass.

McNutt, P.A. (2002). *The Economics of Public Choice*, second edition. Cheltenham, UK: Edward Elgar Publishing.

McNutt, P.A. (2003). Taxonomy of non-market economics for European competition policy. *World Competition*, Vol. 26, pp. 303–332.

McNutt, P.A. (2005). *Law, Economics and Antitrust*. Cheltenham, UK: Edward Elgar Publishing.

McNutt, P.A. (2008). *Signalling, Strategy and Management Type*. E-book, available on www.patrickmcnutt.com.

McNutt, P.A. (2009). Secrets and lies: the neighbourhood of no-truth. *Homo Oeconomicus*, Vol. 26, pp. 161–171.

McNutt, P.A. (2010a). *Game Embedded Strategy*. Singapore: McGraw-Hill.

McNutt, P.A. (2010b). *Political Economy of Law*. Cheltenham, UK: Edward Elgar Publishing.

Mischel, W. (1968). *Personality and Assessment*. Hoboken, NJ: John Wiley & Sons.

Monsen Jr., R.J. and A. Downs. (1965). A theory of large managerial firms. *Journal of Political Economy*, Vol. 73, pp. 221–236.

Moore, H.L. (1906). Paradoxes of competition. *Quarterly Journal of Economics*, Vol. 20, pp. 211–231.

Moore, P.G. and H. Thomas (1976). *The Anatomy of Decisions*. London: Penguin Books.

Mueller, D.C. (1972). A life cycle theory of the firm. *Journal of Industrial Economics*, Vol. 20, pp. 199–219.

Mun, T. (1664). *England's Treasure by Foreign Trade*. Essex, UK: Drury Rare Books.

Nalebuff, B.J and A.K. Dixit. (2008). *The Art of Strategy: A Game Theorist's Guide to Success in Business and Life*. New York: W.W. Norton & Company.

Nash Jr., J.F. (1950). The bargaining problem. *Econometrica*, Vol. 18, pp. 155–162.

Nolan, R.L. and D.C. Croson. (1995). *Creative Destruction*. Cambridge, MA: Harvard University Press.

Owen, G. (1982). *Game Theory*. New York: Academic Press.

Page, G. (1999). *The Singing Gorilla: Understanding Animal Intelligence*. London: Headline Book Publishing.

Penrose, E. (1959). *The Theory of the Growth of the Firm*. New York: Oxford University Press.

Pesendorfer, W. (2006). Behavioural economics comes of age: a review essay on advances in behavioral economics. *Journal of Economic Literature*, Vol. 44, pp. 712–731.

Price, G. (1970). Selection and covariance. *Nature*, Vol. 227, pp. 520–527.

Reny P.J. (1993). Common belief and the theory of games with perfect information. *Journal of Economic Theory*, Vol. 59, pp. 257–274.

Samuelson, L. (2005). Foundations of human sociality: a review essay. *Journal of Economic Literature*, June 2005, Vol. 43, pp. 488–497.

Schelling, T. (1960). *The Strategy of Conflict*. Cambridge, MA: Harvard University Press.

Scherer, F.M. and D. Ross. (1990). *Industrial Market Structure and Economic Performance*. Chicago: Rand McNally.

Schmalensee, R. (1979). *Economics of Advertising*. Amsterdam and New York: North Holland Publishers.

Schumpeter, J. (1934). *The Theory of Economic Development*. Cambridge, MA: Harvard University Press.

Scouller, J. (2005). *Marris Model of the Firm*. University of Strathclyde, mimeo.

Selten, R. (1991). Properties of a measure of predictive success. *Mathematical Social Sciences*, Vol. 21, pp. 153–167.

Shubik, M. (1960). *The Meaning of Modern Business*. New York: Columbia University Press.

Sraffa, P. (1925). On the relation between costs and quantity produced [in Italian]. *The Economic Journal*, December, pp. 277–328.

Stigler, G. (1964). A theory of oligopoly. *Journal of Political Economy*, Vol. 72, pp. 44–61.

Taleb, N.N. (2007). *The Black Swan*. New York: Random House.

Taylor, A.D. and A.M. Pacelli. (2008). *Mathematics and Politics: Strategy, Voting, Power, and Proof*, second edition. New York: Springer.

Tremblay, V. (1987). Scale economies, technological change, and firm cost asymmetries in the U.S. brewing industry. *Quarterly Review of Economics and Business*, Vol. 27, pp. 71–86.

Varley, G.C. (1973). *Insect Population Ecology: An Analytical Approach*. Oxford: Blackwell.

Vives, X. (2005). Complementarities and games: new developments. *Journal of Economic Literature*, Vol. 43, pp. 437–479.

Von Neumann, J. and O. Morgenstern. (1944). *Theory of Games and Economic Behaviour*. Princeton, NJ: Princeton University Press.

Williamson, O. (1971). The vertical integration of production. *American Economic Review*, Vol. 61, pp. 112–123.

Wilson, R. (1991). Multi-product tariffs. *Journal of Regulatory Economics*, Vol. 3, pp. 5–26.

Zitzewitz, E. (2012). Forensic economics. *Journal of Economic Literature*, Vol. 50, pp. 731–769.

Index